THE
Dyslexic
Healer

*Brings ancient shamanic
skills into modern times*

Susan Martin

HEARTSPIRIT

The author of this book does not dispense medical advice or advise the use of techniques shown in this book for any form of treatment. The tools shown in this book are for example only. They are not intended by the author to be a substitute for any licensed professional's advice or treatments. In the event you use any of the information contained in this book for yourself, the author and publisher assume no responsibility for your actions.

The Dyslexic Healer Copyright © 2022 Susan Beth Martin

First paperback edition March 2022

Cover Photographer: Pedro Malacas
Back Cover Photographer: Gene Murrieta
Editors: Dr. Ernie Almendarez, Annie J,
Padmini Grace Covault, and Joe Pierson
Book Design: Shelby Gates

ISBN: 978-0-578-36184-0

Published by Kindle Direct Publishing

For my fifth-grade teacher,
Pastor Robert L. Brown

TABLE *of* CONTENTS

Author's Note..7

Introduction 9

Chapter 1: The Crow 19

Chapter 2: Warrior in the Making 47

Chapter 3: The Channel..........................89

Chapter 4: Native American Sweat Lodge 113

Chapter 5: Cairns................................125

Chapter 6: End of May..........................149

Chapter 7: Miracles Happen 193

Acknowledgements 201

AUTHOR'S NOTE

This is the story of how I was seeking to heal my body with movement. Miraculously, I was shown my abilities as a spiritual healer, leader, and teacher.

I now feel writing, my former nemesis, is like making art. I have always made art by finding a quiet space and letting my mind and hands flow. I understood that I was tapping my brain into the mind of infinite intelligence. But now, because of trainings with my many amazing masters, mentors, and teachers, I've mastered tapping into the Divine with clarity.

This is the story of realizing that I have a connection with the Divine, and how it is for me to live a life with this connection; the story of how the unseen world became my real world. I was guided by metaphysical beings, to share this story to show people a different way to live.

INTRODUCTION

I'm sitting quietly in my fifth-grade classroom, dressed in a surfer-style graphic T-shirt and baggy Levi's that hang low, below my waist in the fashion of the time. Thirty-two other students and I are seated in rows of light-colored wooden desks in an overcrowded Southern California public school.

Our teacher was small in stature, a Black man named Mr. Brown. His dark-colored sport coat hung a little too long in the jacket and sleeves. Then, the extra length of fabric from his matching slacks piled up on the tops of his shoes. His back was to us as he drew with white chalk on the large blackboard, the screech of the soft chalk as his hand tapped and scraped quickly across the board pervading our sensitive ears. He was talking as he wrote, but I had stopped listening to the words; it was all just too confusing.

My eyes wandered, as usual, and this time I was looking at a girl's braided hair to my right, thinking about how her mother must have brushed and separated it. I wondered if her mom pulled her head around as she combed it back to collect it in her hands, causing her to wince, like my mother used to do. Last year, to save myself from the unwanted attention from my mother, I had asked for my long brown hair to be cut in a bob just below my chin.

On this morning, I had made my own breakfast, a can of Campbell's soup—my alternating favorite being scrambled eggs. I'd also run a brush through my straight short hair, and then I set off to walk around the block to meet up with my best friend, Susie; together, we would walk our usual half mile to school.

As for my mother, well, I hadn't seen any sign of her in months.

Dad was doing the best he could, and lately, he'd taken me shopping at Sears and Roebuck, best known for being a catalog store for remote areas and mainly a great store to shop for Craftsman tools, appliances, and lawn mowers. But for dresses? I tried not to complain, but these dresses were really dumb. Dresses with buttons that didn't even function, just sewn on for decoration. I had fashion flair. I loved to hang out with Sylvia, my hipster grandmother, who dressed in the cool late-sixties fringe and velvet. I knew the difference between well-fashioned dresses and shabby substitutes, even at this young age. These inexpensive dresses were my dad's solution to a back-to-school wardrobe. I lived in East County San Diego in the small community of La Mesa, which was always hot right into late October, so these lightweight permanent-press dresses were useful for a while, but once the air cooled, I switched to wearing Levi's, T-shirts, and a zipped hoodie sweatshirt until spring.

These trendy fashions were provided at Christmas by a very practical Santa. My mom would wrap up dark-blue shrink-to-fit Levi's, Hang Ten graphic T-shirts with a pocket, and a package of white sweat socks. So, I did appreciate my father's effort to actually take me shopping for back-to-school clothes, instead of waiting for Christmas.

Dress codes were evolving in the 1970s; the days of girls on their knees to make sure their dresses touched the ground were gone. This was the first year at my grammar school in which we were allowed to wear blue jeans to class, so I was digging that, but even then, it seemed I couldn't get the dress code right. I had recently gotten sent home for wearing a cropped top that showed one and a half inches of my tan little belly.

So today, I was really trying to stay out of trouble, but this lesson had already lost me. I looked out the classroom windows that reached almost to the ceiling and had to be opened and closed with a long wooden pole with a little brass hook on the end. I reviewed the class's torn-paper art on the corkboards on the other side of the room, then glanced to make sure the teacher's back was still toward me.

Now, I quietly slipped my little black mouse out of my T-shirt pocket into my open-backed desk. Speedy immediately raced around the space that was designed for books, notes, and pencils. I was trying to be very careful not to draw attention to myself. I didn't want to be put outside the classroom onto the patio, or worse yet, to be sent out the front door to sit on the open cement walkway where the sixth graders could clearly see me.

It bothered me to have the older kids see me being punished, because I figured they must have known I'd been a really bad kid to get put out there. But when I was put outside on the other side of the building, the patio side, I faced the younger kids' building. Things were different there. I thought they must be thinking that I was really cool for getting out of class. Although Mr. Brown sent me outside almost every day during math and English, he always brought me back in for the fun parts of the school day.

He would sit me next to him on the piano bench while he played, and I joyfully sang along with him at the top of my lungs. I loved all of the wonderful folk songs telling stories of long ago.

"She'll be coming around the mountain when she comes; she'll be driving six white horses when she comes!"

It was as if the wind was blowing my hair back, and I'd feel the vibration of the hooves pounding into the trail as my team galloped around a mountain bend. I loved feeling the songs come alive in my imagination. The other kids barely opened their mouths to sing, so

I was assuming my teacher appreciated my enthusiasm for his piano playing. I remember him looking down at me with a big smile as if I was his partner in some special secret journey.

I didn't do as well in the subjects of math and English. To me, it all looked like hieroglyphics on the blackboard, and I would get lost halfway through the first sentence of a math word problem. As hard as I tried, I was much too slow at translating the sounds coming out of people's mouths into the pictures of the number symbols in my head and then saving the images and adding the next one.

I would complete the first two numbers and realize everyone else was already finished with the next set. This was very upsetting to me; I knew I was smart and wondered what was going on. Why could they all do problems in their heads but I couldn't?

One day, Mr. Brown kept me after class, and I was writing one hundred times, "I will not talk out of turn in the classroom," and another fifth-grade teacher walked by my desk and looked at my paper.

She said, "You write like a boy."

It was true that I was a bit of a tomboy. I liked roller skating, riding my Stingray bike, and I already knew how to ride the Ace 100cc motorcycle. Also, I confess brushing my hair was never a priority. But despite everything I just mentioned, I admit I took her comment as an insult. I was a girl, and why—because my letters had a variety and inconsistency—was I being accused of writing like a boy? The letters just flowed from my pencil irregularly. That was all. Why was that a boy characteristic?

I also wondered for years why most other girls could make those perfectly uniform letters. As I became more aware in high school, I noticed there were some boys with perfect penmanship too, and it was not a "boy thing," to cross out letters, switch A's for I's, and generally do a lot of scribbling. Now, I realized I was just a messy writer. First off, I was constantly having to guess what the next letter was supposed to be. So, my penmanship had a mixed-up style of constantly switching from script to printing.

High school was not any more satisfying for me than grammar school. The administration had put me into college-prep classes. But I couldn't even read out loud, couldn't spell, and failed ninth-grade algebra. The symbols on the chalkboard switching back and forth were nothing more than a jumbled mess in my mind.

I was kicked out of first-year drama class because I couldn't read out loud. Luckily, there were art classes, and at least I could understand the art teachers. They were a lot less interested in neat writing; they were more about bright paint colors and messy brushstrokes. I painted, built clay boxes and pinched clay bowls with clay. These were things that won me A's. I barely graduated from high school because of lack of attendance, and I know I didn't even understand simple sentence structure or composition of a paragraph.

I tried college, and the sculpting classes brought me two easy A's. I failed typing and had to drop English 101 twice to avoid being failed. The final time, I took the English class *term paper writing*. I was thirty-four years old, and it was in summer school. I was so happy I could completely understand my teacher's perfect diction. She was from India, and her words were clear and slow. Her efforts and my tenacity paid off, and I completed my first term paper with an A. Writing did not come naturally to me. I have, as it was explained by an adviser after testing at the community college, "symbol problems."

Years later, I was sitting at the bar next to Zanna, a coworker and an adventurous gal with a pixie haircut and the demeanor of a fairy.

She inquisitively asked, "Have you been doing Reiki?"

I went deep inside my thoughts, shutting out the loud music and the steamy energy from the patrons at the cabaret as I rolled through the movie of my recent life.

I came up with the disappointing thought of *No*.

But the truth was that almost every day at home in San Diego, I gave Reiki to my dog, myself, and maybe a family member or a close friend.

But Zanna had come to my now-closed office and received professional Reiki healing sessions from me, and I was thinking this is what she must was referring to.

I answered, "No, but I have been working on an interesting healing project that's going to take me to

17

Australia; actually, we have narrowed it down to Cairns for starters."

Zanna reminded me she went to Cairns a few years ago to get a scuba diving certificate. I was intrigued and chatted my plans to her.

I explained, "I have been receiving instructions through tarot card readings and messages from a noisy crow, and this crow has made it known he is conveying a message from Crow Nation."

She told me how Cairns was a strange little town, and the beaches unsafe to go on because the ocean was shallow for long distances and filled with crocodiles. She added that the trees hung their branches low, heavy with bats all day—until sunset, when they'd all suddenly take flight to go hunt in the nearby hills.

I thought, *I can't wait to add this to the story! The place the crow is sending me has crocodile-filled beaches and bat-filled trees.*

CHAPTER 1

The Crow

I stood at the stove, watching breakfast eggs sizzle in a small cast-iron pan. My ex-boyfriend was on his phone in my living room. This storytelling financial adviser would brag to Uber drivers as they drove us from the upscale condo out and about to local restaurants, telling them how it was our place. Well, it wasn't "our place" at all; it was *my* place, one I had secured singlehandedly, with no input from him.

I had returned from India after completing my two-hundred-hour yoga teacher training. I moved from his house into the rented condo. I was seeking ease in my life, and moving back into town felt good. Honestly, we hadn't spent much time together since

I'd moved out, but today we were "playing house," as he liked to call it.

Suddenly, he blurted into his iPhone, "There's some bird outside just going after it! It's really making a racket," ending his comment with a throaty chuckle.

I slid the over-medium eggs onto plates and slathered the sourdough toast with ghee. I listened intently. There was a uniquely clear repetitive clucking sound coming in through the open front door. I walked out onto the covered patio that faced the southeast corner of the picturesque man-made lake. Then my attention was guided by the noisy bird, and I looked up to my right. Sitting on the ledge above me was a large black bird relentlessly clucking away to itself—or to me? It was staring down at me with those shiny little black crow eyes, cocking its head side to side. My nine-pound dog growled, barked, and lunged toward the bird. I quieted my pet and then watched as the crow took flight and landed in one of the sparsely leaf-covered trees that encircled the little half-mile-long lake.

I walked back into the rented condo and admired the golden sunlight dripping onto the antique-filled room. I ate my breakfast, aware of having inquisitive thoughts about the bird. I had heard about crows and messages; was there something the corvid was trying to tell me?

I liked imagining that maybe mystical beings were reaching out to me, and these past few months, things had gotten very interesting. During private healing sessions, I was seeing in my mind's eye and also smelling things that weren't present in the physical world. I watched as healing masters performed extractions and additions of energy in the best interest of my clients. I saw strange creatures representing energy that wasn't theirs, as it left their physical and ethereal bodies. I saw beautiful golden lights and opalescent rainbows surrounding their bodies. One session stands out in my mind, where I was shown in my mind's eye a complete children's book of watercolor nature fairies. I took the time, and I painted a watercolor of one small fairy boy sitting by a pond under a willow and then decided to put the book of watercolor nature fairies aside. I felt it was more important to put together a small self-healing workshop for a few close friends. Whether I was painting or doing group healing work, in general, I was finding the Reiki practice inspirational.

"Have a good day!" I announced, as I hustled out the door heading to the Reiki house. "I'm going to the office. I'm going to give my Reiki master a healing."

After I had finished the Japanese modality of energy work called Reiki for Michael, my master, I walked out to the parking lot behind the office space. The Reiki house was less than a mile from the condo, and I was parked in the far right-hand corner of the lot, one space off the side wall of a flat-roofed, two-story pink cinder-block building.

As I got to my car, I heard that clear clucking sound again and looked up. Perched exactly at the corner of the brick building, and staring right down at me, was a large black bird, rattling loudly.

I chuckled to myself. "So, it's this guy again."

I got into my red Mini Cooper and took a deep breath and thought, but that's more obvious. Now, I'm not at the lake where black birds fill the trees. Here, the corvid's appearance really sparked my curiosity. I had never noticed any big black birds in this area, and he was clucking right at me. *He must really be trying to tell me something* was all I could conclude.

Before I even started my car, I texted my friend Kaylee—a diviner with the gift of magical insight. One tool she practiced with was tarot cards, and she also had her Reiki I and II training.

"Can we please meet tomorrow? I want healing and a tarot card reading; it looks like some crow is trying to talk to me, and I don't understand him, and he is really trying hard. I'm wondering if he has an important message for me."

I sent a similar text to my Reiki master, Michael. They both replied quickly, and we set an appointment to meet at the Reiki house for the next day.

I wasn't disappointed with the healing they gave me; it was a delightful dual Reiki session, and the Divine poured through them. I was totally relaxed, and we had moved from the treatment room into the reception area. We were all seated at a large, heavy wooden desk in the front room of the office. Kaylee, still in her twenties and alive with young charm, had also been blessed with enough aesthetically pleasing features and height that in her late teens she had been a professional runway model. She sat with her calm demeanor and earned confidence across the desk from Michael and me. Because I'd never had a tarot card reading, I was both excited and nervous.

I asked, "What is the crow trying to tell me?"

The cards showed pictures that told a story to Kaylee, explaining that I was to travel and do healing work, and by this time next year, I should shut down my condo. They said I would be traveling so much, I would not even know where my home was, and so I really wouldn't have any need for a place of my own. This was exciting to me, as I'd always been a great traveler. My mind raced with thoughts of traveling to all kinds of exotic places: Peru for plant medicine, the Caribbean for scuba diving, Tibet for spiritual work, or perhaps Japan for William Lee Rand's Advanced Reiki Training?

We asked about me doing plant medicine ritual, and I was warned it could be dangerous for me to go to Peru, but it may be okay for me to do plant medicine in Costa Rica or California. We also asked about the financial advisor, and he was shown providing assistance to me with a journey. Then, we were told, he would do something that would really make me angry near the end of that year, and that I would soon totally stop talking to him. I found myself feeling intrigued. How could a guy that I had already broken up with three years ago piss me off any worse than he already had? But I was delighted with the foreshadowing of travel and adventure.

Michael and Kaylee seemed a little disturbed, and they expressed concern.

"Where are you going to go?" Kaylee whined. "I don't want you to leave."

"I can't do this by myself. I need you here, Susie," Michael huffed.

I responded with, "Oh, guys, the end of next year is a long time away."

I was thinking that closing down my home, with more than thirty years of collected antiques and art, would be an interesting challenge in itself. Feeling the love of these two amazing healers and realizing how important I had become to them in such a short time felt really good. How will I be able to leave?

Everything had been going so well. Michael had scheduled my Reiki I and II training at convenient midday, midweek times that I had available. I had wanted to do these classes while I was completing my three-hundred-hour yoga-teacher training, but I'd been unable to fit the weekend trainings offered into my full weekend work schedule.

As I studied with Michael, he expressed how special my healings felt and immediately scheduled me in with his wife and a week later with an out-of-town Reiki master. The master had seen our office as he drove by. He was in town from Texas to help his grandmother with some yard work.

I arrived at my appointment to practice Reiki on the master as Michael and the master were chatting in the reception area. I was introduced, and I noticed how handsome the senior master was. I didn't ask any questions such as, *What is going on with you?* or *What kind of healing are you seeking?* Instead, I just blindly went into the treatment room. I had been doing energy work for five years, and I had learned to ground myself before and after I worked. I felt relaxed and ready.

The master climbed onto the Reiki table, basically a massage table. I prepared the room energetically, using my newly learned Reiki I and II tools. Except, no one had shown me to use my jewelry in a healing session, but today I did. I laid my White Buffalo turquoise-and-silver Navajo-made necklace on his forehead. Then, placing my hands gently over his ears, I felt my hands quickly warm and tingle. After a few moments, I moved my hands in traditional Reiki hand placements to his shoulders, his chest, and then his digestive organs.

As I reached his hips, my body warmed, and I thought this must be a hormonal hot flash. I felt my body heat up and told myself, *don't be a baby, it will pass.* But it didn't. Suddenly, I felt like my organs were going to implode. It felt as if there was a volcano pouring out hot lava inside of me. I pulled away and got down on my knees, connecting my hands with the earth, and then I pushed back, connecting my hips onto my heels, into a very grounding yoga pose. My body cooled as it connected to the earth's energy, and I returned to my work. But again I started to overheat. So, I pulled away and again went down onto the floor to cool. Then I decided not to try working on his lower body again. I headed up the left side, stopping at his arm. Worried that I would overheat again, I kneeled with my head resting on my right arm. I wished for the energy to run cold. Instantly, I felt a coolness rush through my body. I thought, *that was different.*

After the session, we chatted. He had done his training in Japan and practiced in France for fifteen years. I couldn't help but think how amazing it was that a guy like this would show up in my second week of Reiki practice. I explained to him what had happened during the session. He looked at me with dark, soft eyes that invited my stare.

He spoke. "Think of yourself as a big rock in a river. You don't move, and the water rushes around and over you, but you are attached to the earth. The water is the energy rushing by. It collects the negative things coming out of the client, so let it rush by, and don't catch any of it. You will work on sick people, people with cancer. You do not want that stuff to stick to you, so just let it flow by."

I listened, and from then on, I practiced with that intention.

A few weeks later, Michael gave me my master attunement, and in the next ten months, I worked on dozens of clients for many hours. If I wanted to do three hours of healing work in a week, I found the spaces were filled. If I desired three hours of healing work in one day, the spaces filled. I felt like I would barely set the intention, and the sessions would become complete.

At the end of February, Kaylee and I went to San Diego, where we attended a shamanic workshop.

I was a little surprised when our teacher immediately asked us to call in our compassionate spirit helpers. I wondered, how did he know we worked with spirit helpers? I enjoyed the weekend workshop in which we did drug-free journeys, drumming, and rattling. I was surprised most of us had drums with us. Mine was a self-made eighteen-inch wood round with deerskin stretched over it, that I had adorned with a pencil drawing of a wolf. I had made my tom-tom for striking the drum with a willow stick wrapped in fabrics.

The intro to the Foundation workshop taught by Juan Carlos Safa had attracted other already-practicing healers, and we gathered power animals from the lower world, dancing with them. We interacted with them, talked to them—and they communicated back to us. Sitting in class, I suddenly got a very clear awareness in my mind of the words "Palo Santo."

I had heard of it before, but I didn't know it was for clearing negative energies. I decided I must have a spirit guide who liked the scent, and I was unaware of how powerful the scent was and how I would use it in the future in my protection fragrances and ceremonial sprays.

The journeying during the workshop was the most memorable part. I lay there on the floor, listening to the drum beating, the action in my mind's eye becoming very clear and vivid. I could see plants growing up rapidly like a dense jungle, then completing their life cycle, withering to dust, and then I would see only dirt. This all appeared so vividly, it was like I was watching an animated movie in my mind. About the fifth time I was shown this same scene, I asked for it to stop. I felt I had gotten the message—destroy all that exists now, and it will grow back new and strong.

Everything from the card reading and the messages Kaylee had received from the crow was starting to come true. I was traveling and learning new healing skills. I was now convinced that I didn't need plant medicine to be able to experience powerful shamanic journeys. I thought that journey was so vivid! What if I would've been on a journey with plant medicine? How would I have been able to ask it to stop?

The six months that I needed to complete practicing Reiki healings before attending the Advanced Reiki Training passed quickly. I had been planning to attend the workshop in Redondo Beach, but it would have been a very expensive trip without the convenience of my ex's condo. So, I had not signed up for the training. But unexpectedly, a few days before the March start date of the workshop, Sean contacted me out of the blue. He invited me to Redondo, and he bought me a plane ticket to LA. Kaylee's reading was true again. Although we hadn't even been talking, he had assisted me on my path.

The day before I left for Southern California, Kaylee's eleven-year-old son read Native American tarot cards for me.

"What's the deal with the crow giving me messages?" I asked, looking for more clarity on the crow spirit guide.

Seated across from me on the oversized sectional couch, Evan shuffled his deck and carefully placed a face-down row of cards.

As he flipped each card up, he spoke. "He has been looking for you for a long time, and when he was looking for you, he found others that were looking for you."

I thought, *the crow must not be the only one with a message for me.* But I was more interested in tomorrow's adventure.

I asked, "What about this Advanced Reiki Training I'm going to Redondo Beach for, will it be good for me?"

Evan answered, "You are going to up level your skills."

I had researched this class months before and was aware that this attunement would come directly through Jesus to us students. It sure did sound like up leveling to me.

I didn't think or plan any of it; it seemed everything just happened. I booked the workshop two days before it started, and suddenly, I was walking the one-mile trek along the beach to take part in it. The other side, the energetic part of life, was really getting my attention. I didn't need to plan. Everything flowed, and it was all so real. My guides had taken over, and I was just strapped in for the ride.

All of this was still fairly new to me. My first experience with interacting with a guide had been in 2012. I had been seated in the yoga room with my study group formed by Art Runningbear, and someone had brought a message to the group that in the valley there was an evil dragon terrorizing families. I suspected dark arts, but any prior knowledge of these modalities only came from timelines of past lives. I'd never had any interest in anything dark in this lifetime. Honestly, at the point at which I was working with this group, I was basically afraid of everything.

Anyway, in this meeting, someone mentioned crystal dragons, and I was engaged immediately; that was the coolest thing I had ever heard of. Crystal dragons! I closed my eyes. I still wasn't brave enough to close my eyes and sit still at home by myself, but with my group, I felt safe. We would create a dome of protection, ground our room and ourselves, and then go into meditation with some job to do. In my imagination, everything flowed and was very clear. It was like being an actor in a movie. I flew straight up above the school, where I saw myself, sword and shield in hand, my long blonde hair braided into two tails. I saw three white dragons in front of me. Suddenly, I heard a loud, booming voice coming from my right. I looked and saw a big hunk of a man dressed as a warrior.

"It's so good to see you!" the enormous sexy guy roared as he picked me up and gave me a huge hug.

I giggled in real life, and thought, *wow, I have some imagination.* I didn't realize I was walking on the other side or that I was working with a spirit guide to defeat evil.

Now here in Redondo Beach, the Advanced Reiki Training and Master Level of the Usui Holy Fire II Workshop, hosted by William Lee Rand began with dancing to shamanic drumming music. I was pleasantly surprised by this. I had not expected Reiki training to include dancing and drumming. He also explained how we were expected to only use third-heaven spirit guides with this practice. Personally, I wasn't even aware that I was using spirit guides in Reiki healings. I thought I'd only been working with God or the Divine.

However, a channel in Sedona had given me special instructions to work with the "Rainbow Healers of Light" for a healing specific to Kaylee's partner. The channel had also introduced me to the ascended master, Hilarion. He was who I had been consulting for clarity on truths current and future.

Runningbear had told us when practicing healing on someone, we must always give any helpers that we asked for assistance a time limit, so they wouldn't be hanging around in our space when we weren't doing healings. Because I used this time-limit practice, I always felt safe calling on helpers.

Since my Reiki master training, I'd solely used sacred Reiki symbols during healing sessions, and I had not been using spirit guides. But when Senior Master William Lee Rand asked us, for the time being, to disconnect from our current guides, I saw Hilarion calmly and graciously bow his head to me and turn away. Jesus was introduced for the attunement, and he was used exclusively in the practice taught that weekend. We were taught a new-to-me extraction method with the assistance of Jesus, and during this training, I physically felt things leaving my body. Although I had slept through a lot of the instruction, I still gained all the knowledge I needed, as the training was powerful.

✦

I went back home and continued doing plenty of healing work and teaching Reiki. After the advanced training, teaching these classes now came easily, Senior Master William Lee Rand's well-organized manuals making the task of teaching the classes simple.

The attunement was coming directly from Jesus; without the Reiki attunement passing through a human master, it was powerful. The extraction method the Senior Master had taught in his advanced training worked well. I was seeing good results with clients. I actually started seeing too much during healing sessions and began asking not to be shown what was coming out of my clients.

This was also when I started teaching yoga to the kids. Honestly, as I write this, my eyes are welling with tears, the memory of the classes I taught to them that spring touching my heart. My fondest memory is of seventeen elementary students standing in a circle with their hands at their hearts in prayer, some with heads down and eyes closed. At first, it was a little out of my comfort zone to teach children, but then I was so well received. The namaste song with hand gestures was their favorite time during class.

"When is the namaste song?" a student asked.

"It's what we sing at the very end of our class," I answered.

I loved that they remembered the song where we honored each other with each other's light.

As my year played out, my paying healing clients had become a steady stream, and I was also teaching gentle yoga on Saturdays. I enjoyed walking the lake park in front of my condo, swimming laps in the community pool, and traveling just a bit. I love outdoor swimming during the summer, and I wanted to enjoy it as much as possible.

But at the same time, I knew I was also moving back home to San Diego. I could feel the energy in my life shifting as my furniture started moving out the door. I would sit in amazement and wonder if I could

really do this, actually release 95 percent of my belongings and move into a bedroom back in the house
I'd grown up in.

Of course, I also had an annoying sibling who
tried to insinuate I was having a hard time in my life
and that this was why I was moving home. It actually
makes me snicker as I write this. It was difficult for me
to stay in heart and not let outside influences affect
my decisions, and I definitely wasn't immune to her
comments. I almost canceled my whole idea of closing
down my home, thinking, *why would I give up my easy,
miraculous life in this fun town to go to a city with traffic
and pollution?* Why give up my noncommittal life of
getting up when I wanted, working when I wanted,
basically doing everything and anything I wanted. But
by now I was determined, and I stuck with my plans to
get to spend time with my aging parents. I was looking
forward to exploring why I was guided by a crow to
close down my home and travel.

The move went well, only because Kim and Mary—
Kim being my childhood neighbor and most supportive
friend over the last twenty years, and Mary a friend of

fifteen years whom I'd met during my residential real estate practice flew in together from San Diego.

I had introduced Mary to my high-school buddy Michael, and he had given her a job. This had made it possible for her to move to San Diego five years prior. I literally worked at the restaurant right up to the very last night. So, Kim was at the house, packing for me. I could feel the weight falling off of me. I was committed, and I was moving into my ninety-year-old parents' house. No more wondering if they were okay. No more feeling lonely in the condo six hundred miles away from my family. I was taking my dog and going there, and it felt great.

I would randomly tell people, "I do have a mom and dad; I wasn't hatched from an egg."

On October 15, 2018, just as planned, we finished up with all the packing. Mary took off in the rental moving truck, to clean out her storage space she had left behind five years earlier; then she headed to San Diego. I bought Kim a plane ticket on Southwest Airlines to fly her home, sparing her the drive. Then I stuffed the last of my clothes and hangers into the red Mini Cooper and headed to San Diego myself.

It was rough for Mom as my belongings arrived. Mom couldn't stand any stuff, never mind other people's stuff. I had attempted to really streamline all my belongings for my own sanity. But I really still felt like I had too much junk. It was tough sizing down to a guest room at my parents' when I'd been living on my own in large homes most of the last twenty-three years.

I was still on the road when Mary arrived, backing the huge truck into the driveway. But luckily, my brother just happened to be at my parents' place. So, Mary and Lance worked together like a professional loading dock crew. They emptied the rented box truck and filled the Mini Cooper's soon-to-be parking spot in the garage. The pile of my stuff was high and wide, and there were at least six large boxes marked to go to Kim's. These were treasures, an extra-large Kitchen Aid, mixing bowls, and a mass of cookware she was gladly inheriting. I had some necessities—my Vitamix blender and a Nespresso machine—that I added to my mother's already-complete kitchen.

Mom's eyes grew big every time I brought yet another box of clothes into the house. I had given away and sold so much stuff but still had a lot of designer shoes and clothing items that I just wasn't ready to part with. So, I stuffed the small closet of the 1964 house with woolen suits, sweaters, and cocktail dresses. Why I thought I was going to need these items in San Diego wasn't clear, but I had already given up most of thirty years of collected antiques and treasures to fit back into the spare bedroom of the 1,600-square-foot tract home.

I was just so thankful they had finally added air-conditioning. Living in East County San Diego without air-conditioning was impossible. It gets hot, over a hundred degrees, and humid, and I can remember being completely immobile living in houses in San Diego without air-conditioning back in the eighties. I would lie on the couch, nauseated from the heat and wondering what I needed to do to be rich enough to afford air-conditioning.

I had gone out in the world, made money, and lived twenty-three years with air-conditioning and whatever else I wanted. But now, here I was, back in my parents' home in La Mesa, eager to find out the real why and excited to experience my changing life.

The why became very clear as my heart filled with love, getting up in the morning with my mother, Annie, making her a cup of Nespresso coffee with whipped milk.

"Good morning, Mama. How are you today?"

"Oh, I'm okay. Is the coffee shop open?"

"Yes, Mama. Would you like a vanilla latte today? Or do you want to sample the Cuban blend?"

"Oh, that Cuban sounds like good coffee."

"Okay, Mama, Cuban it is!"

I would go into the kitchen and start the coffee and the milk frothing, then go back into the living room to make small talk with Annie. I'd zip back into the kitchen and pour the hot whipped milk into the crema created by the Nespresso coffeemaker. This filled the large mug almost to the top. Finally, I proudly presented the hot latte to my Mama.

"Done already, and I didn't even know you were making it! Oh look, there's an angel! Oh, Susie, you gotta see this; there's really an angel in my coffee cup!"

She would show me the foam of the hot drink, take a big swallow, then usually say the same thing all over again. "That's really good coffee."

Then she would add, "Oh, you make me good coffee."

My heart would smile. She was so easy to make happy, and it was clear why I was there. Actually, Mom and Dad were both happy to have me around the place, whipping up meals, food shopping, visiting with them, listening to stories of their youth. They also really loved having Peanut the dog there, and he had fallen in love with both of them. As a nine-pound dog, he took full advantage of the available laps.

Being in San Diego gave me access to more Shamanic workshops. An extraction workshop was the second one I took. I was standing behind a classmate, my mind blank, and scolded myself—I'm so bad at this! I never get auditory messages, never mind a song. Then I got a knowing, sing a song you know!

"I've got peace like a river in my soul."

My classmate asked after I was done, "Did you know that song?"

I said, "Yeah, I sing it with the kids when I teach them yoga for my after-school program." The truth was I hadn't felt comfortable enough to sing the howling sounds that I normally would sing when alone with my drum. We all switched, and it was my turn to be sung to. The sounds were unusual.

I didn't know what they were, and when I asked, she said, "The whale song. They said you would know what that means."

I smiled, knowing exactly what that meant. Right after we'd learned how to channel in Sedona, Kaylee had asked me to channel that exact question.

"What does the whale song mean?"

"Love," had been the answer then.

My classmate's song was amazing, and I felt like a different person than before she started, going from mind-scattered to perfectly calm. The assignment had been to go to the lower world, meet with a spirit guide and let them sing a song to you, and then sing to your practice client. I felt like I had failed and my classmate had succeeded.

But where I really succeeded in this class was in creating a ceremonial extraction scent. After the first meeting on Saturday, I went home and opened my perfume box, dropping into a trance and asking for all the spirit guides of the other students from the class to join me in my room. I looked across the bedroom, and it was as if I could see an energy. No outline, nothing physical, just some kind of jumping energy.

I spoke to that energy, "Okay, tell me what it is you'd like me to put into this extraction fragrance."

I was clearly directed by the spirit guide to use these four items from my collection of resins and oils, copal, African sandalwood, cedarwood, and bergamot. I thought this was an incomplete formula.

So, I asked, "Can I add a little patchouli?"

I received a big *"No!"*

"How about lavender?"

Again, I received the message of "No!"

The next day, I returned to the class with five-milliliter roll-ons of the custom combination for the extraction class. I had clearly listed on my business card what I had put into the scent.

One of my classmates read it carefully and then looked at me and said, "I had a spirit guide asking me for this combination, and I was wondering where I was going to get it."

That explained why I had heard the combination so clearly. Then as we broke for lunch, another classmate—a massage therapist—decided it was very important to tell me how much she despised patchouli and lavender. So funny. But this gave me confidence that I was getting accurate messages from the metaphysical world.

CHAPTER 2

Warrior in the Making

I slowly transformed from the fear of hearing or seeing messages from realities beyond, to taking to heart and acting on messages possibly coming from different dimensions.

I didn't just wake up one day and say, "Hey, I'm connected with the metaphysical. I get messages out of thin air, listen to crows, and can move energy in the metaphysical world—and change things in the physical world!"

It didn't go quite like that; as with most skills, it was acquired over time, and it was learned. I'm not certain when the journey began, but in the year 2000, I unintentionally added the discipline of stillness to my life.

Going as far back as the early nineties, however, I'd already had some strange, unexplainable, drug-free experiences, such as a red glowing ball showing itself to me in my bedroom, and also someone performing a mind-blowing spiritual surgery on me.

But to keep the story of my progression more concrete, we will start with me adding yoga to my week. At this time, I was living in a spacious vaulted-ceiling condominium with a view of the entire valley. I had hired a yoga instructor to come twice a week in the late mornings for private yoga lessons, and to be truthful, I found the practice he instructed a bit annoying. I felt like it was a waste of time lying there with my hands in a triangle shape on my belly, or sitting in an awkward position, cross-legged and seated with my hands in prayer in front of my chest. Honestly, I hated sitting still. However, I loved the stretching of my tight muscles, and also found the time spent sitting and lying around somehow made it easier to deal with people and their moods.

For the next ten years, I was more interested in weightlifting, eating well, and drinking a little wine. It wasn't until 2010 that I really had any kind of consistent yoga practice. That year, I attended more than 120 ninety-minute classes of the Bikram hot yoga method. I loved the sweating and also found that I loved developing discipline; it takes a lot of attention to what you are eating and drinking to practice yoga in a 105-degree room day after day. The highly energetic practice took my mind off the outside world; it was fair to say that by now, yoga had gotten my attention, and I was feeling the changes both in my body and mind.

As the calendar year moved into 2012, I found myself living in my little rental house. I had just claimed bankruptcy, resulting from over-leveraging myself with real-estate investment loans. This house was really all I had, and because of a huge market dip, there wasn't any equity in it. So luckily, in bankruptcy, I could keep as my personal residence. It was just far enough away from my acquaintances that I found I had a little more personal time. I hired a trainer and added weightlifting into my afternoons. My body was sore and stiff and craving yoga.

One Monday afternoon in October 2012, I opened my brand-new laptop. In the previous ten days, I had downloaded the Netflix streaming app and watched two quantum-physics movies, a documentary on ayahuasca, and enjoyed other assorted movies about nature and nutrition. But today, I Googled *yoga classes*, and the results showed one studio with a 6 p.m. class in the small town about nine miles south of me.

It was a country drive, mostly open space with cattle and horse ranches. As I was driving along the two-lane highway lined with tall trees, I spotted a hawk perched on the top of a telephone pole. But most of the drive, the soft blue skies laced with tic-tac-toe jet contrails had my attention.

I entered the studio. I smelled this amazing, sweet citrus-and-clove scent. It was a lot different from those ill-scented hot yoga classes that I was accustomed to. I also experienced the pose "downward dog" for the first time, named after the way a dog naturally stretches its entire body. You are inverted but still have your feet and hands on the floor. I enjoyed the strength-building poses in this (new-to-me) style of yoga. The teacher kept us moving and breathing as we flowed from one pose to the next. I recognized some of the poses. However, there wasn't the intense heat or long holds of the Bikram practice, and it wasn't as slow and boring as the yoga instruction had been in my living room. It seemed I had really hit a sweet spot, a place that felt good.

Our teacher, Kerry, was a cool middle-aged gal with an outdoorsy look of tanned skin and frosty blonde hair. She sat cross-legged on a rubber mat laid out on the sweet-smelling bamboo floor. Kerry closed the class with a somewhat traditional way of pitching workshops that the studio would be hosting in the near future. "Next weekend, we have a shaman coming."

I was intrigued, my imagination creating a character wearing brightly colored clothes, with painted stripes on his face and feathers coming out the top of his head. I drove home excited. I imagined it was totally reasonable that I was living in Indian Hills and was about to meet an Indian shaman. As soon as I got back home, I opened my laptop to the yoga school website and signed up for the upcoming workshop. For the next two weeks, I did quite a few classes at the studio, and I liked the style of the flowing poses. I also enjoyed the relaxed atmosphere of the school, which reflected the owner, Kerry. She turned out to be a well-traveled lady, a mother and wife of a family of four.

The Saturday morning workshop with the shaman arrived quickly. I had been sound asleep after working the Friday night shift and was awakened by my cell phone. I looked at it and saw the time was 10 a.m. Strange, as no one was on the line when I answered. I truly thought, *why is the universe waking me up so early?* Then I remembered this was the day I was to attend the shaman's workshop. I questioned my sanity as I thought maybe he was that powerful, he could make my cell phone ring! Exhausted, I created the thought that the class was not starting till 11:30 a.m. and closed my eyes, resting for another forty-five minutes.

As I pulled out of the driveway, my cell phone rang again.

I answered, "Hello?"

"Hello, is this Susan Martin?" asked a woman's voice in a scolding tone.

I answered, "Yes." I paused and then asked, "Did the workshop start at eleven o'clock?"

The lady sounded quite irritated by my question

and said, "Yes, but go ahead and come anyways."

The quiet drive to the studio was enjoyable; not normally up this early, I experienced a fresh view of the highway and ranchlands. Being as quiet as possible, I walked into the yoga studio, but it looked and felt different. There was a half-circle of about ten folding chairs with people seated in them, while behind each chair was another person with their hands placed on the seated person's shoulders. I tensed up, my first thought being, *what kind of cult meeting have I shown up for?*

Then immediately I relaxed. I remembered a few years back, two Hare Krishna devotees had given hands-on energy work to me and a boyfriend in Maui, Hawaii. This looked the same, but I was confused. I wondered, *why are we doing this?* My understanding by the end of that first day was it was a cosmic energy we were bringing to each other for a body healing. I thought, *that seems safe enough.*

The weekend moved on, and I was delighted. I felt as if I'd landed in some kind of wonderful metaphysical kindergarten. The skills were simple, and I took to them easily. I felt comfortable. I was glad I had recently watched the quantum-physics movies and a program about plant medicine. The somewhat abstract concepts of the weekend seemed to follow along with my recent Netflix entertainment.

The "shaman" was a Native American healer born into the Apache, called Art Runningbear. He didn't call himself a shaman, and I learned that Shamanic practitioners commonly don't use the term. Instead, he called himself a seer, a medicine man, and a healer. To me, he looked like a regular guy. There was no paint on his face and no feathers on his head, a little disappointing. He was usually wearing a Hawaiian shirt, and we learned that he also practiced his healing methods and teachings in Hawaii. It wasn't in any of his literature, but he did mention when in Hawaii he was called a Kahuna. I learned from Kerry to lightheartedly call him our guru.

We were introduced to skills that brought our awareness to the metaphysical world. We tested our abilities to see and feel the unseen world. We combed, brushed, and fluffed the seven layers of the etheric fields that surrounded our physical bodies. We would feel the vibrations and warmth as we explored the auras around each other. We imagined each other in a glass box and then let the person disappear in our imagination and vacuumed any strange dark spots or gray areas in the glass box away with our imaginary cosmic vacuums. We were introduced to running an imaginary ball of energy from the tops of our heads, down the backs of our spines, around the base of our tailbones, and up the front of us, then back out the tops of our heads.

The first time I attempted this in my imagination, I was watching the ball of light travel down my back, but when I got to my sacrum, the ball of light stopped. I had to repeatedly back it up and try again, and finally it flowed through, but then it got stuck on the belly too. I pushed it up and through the blockages, and it came out the top of my head, and I repeated the exercise. Runningbear told us this skill cleared experiences. He also explained that experiences were karma. He said our bodies held experiences within our etheric body, the chakras, and the aura.

Since then, I've learned the chakras are energy centers within the physical body. These chakras connect us to the metaphysical. The chakras vitalize the physical body with the life-force energy that comes to us from the Divine. I believe our bodies operate a lot better when we clear all foreign entities. Stuff like low-vibration energy, negative experiences, and anyone else's energy can block the energetic channels of the body. After clearing any stuff that does not serve an individual's highest good. I've been taught to then refill all parts of the body with divine life force, cosmic energy, or the individual's own life force.

As Vessa, the director of Intuitive Insights School of Intuition, says, "It's not that these foreign energies are good or bad, it's just that it is not yours."

Runningbear was teaching us valuable basic skills for clearing things from our etheric bodies that no longer served us. This practice assists in creating healthier physical bodies. We were being introduced to an energetic healing practice.

Runningbear held his hands about ten inches apart. "Move your hand through the space between my hands."

As I did this, I could feel a warm, tingling sensation. I·had previously learned in school that there is an electric magnetic field around our bodies, but I always thought our bodies produced it. I was never taught that the energy was coming from the cosmos. I knew some people felt warmer and healthier, and some people colder and not as pleasant to be close to. But I had no idea this energy could be fed to us from the cosmos.

We learned a few intuition-building skills too; one of my favorites was that one person would create an imaginary wall while another would feel the metaphysical wall with their physical hands and describe what they were feeling. We were so surprised by how good we were at this skill. I was paired for the pretend-wall exercise with my soon-to-be-favorite woman of the group, Dianne.

I said, "It feels hard and cold; is it made of ice?"

Dianne said, "Yes, Susie; you got it."

I was amazed and realized very quickly that all those things I'd been feeling around people's bodies all these years were actually real. I felt I was in the right place. Things that I never could make sense of were quickly becoming clearer, and it felt good. We were introduced to clairvoyant skills, meditations, remote viewing, and space clearing.

The highlight of the weekend was that I received some clarity on something that had been going on in my life for the past two years. It was dinner break on Sunday, and I was chatting with a gal who had been my partner on a couple of the skills we had learned that day. I had noticed she was more advanced at what we were doing, and she used words I'd never heard before to describe things that I was doing for the first time. She had complimented me and made me feel great about my abilities. I had not seen her in any of the yoga classes in the last two weeks at the school. So, I asked her how she had found out about the workshop. I listened as she replied.

"I was driving down the road and heard my spirit guides say, 'yoga, yoga, yoga!'

"I responded to them, 'Yes, I know I'm supposed to do yoga, but not right now, I'm busy.'

"But it was nagging at me, so when I got home, I Googled yoga, and this school came up. I assumed there must be some other reason besides yoga. So, I checked workshops, and there it was, Art Runningbear scheduled for that coming weekend. It was Thursday, and I had my weekend well planned out. But still I made a deal with my guides. I'm going on a walk with my dogs, and if you guys give me a sign that this workshop should be a priority, I will adjust my weekend plans and attend. So, I was walking in the forest near my home with my dogs, and I saw a brown bear go running through the trees. I figured that was a clear sign, and I signed up for the workshop with Runningbear."

This story amazed me; she was listening and acting on messages from spirit guides. I thought about my own decision to take the workshop and how I had suddenly had the overpowering need for yoga. I had Googled yoga, and only this school had come up. I went to a yoga class and learned of the upcoming workshop.

I also thought about how two years ago I had sat in my bath and asked the orbs that were flying around my room, "What do you guys want from me? Why are you here?"

I'd received a one-word knowing, "orphans." I decided my classmate might find this story interesting.

I began, "I have these orphan orbs following me around."

As I began, Runningbear joined us at the picnic table.

My classmate looked at him and just like that, said, "He will know what they are."

I felt awkward and that I had been put on the spot, so I kept it short. "I have a friend who was concerned about my well-being, so he sent Indian wolf spirits to protect me. I literally talked to the wolf spirits, and then orbs began flying around my room. Honestly, hundreds of them, and these—totally recordable on video—orbs in various sizes and colors have been following me around for the past two years. I've asked what they were trying to tell me, and the only message I've gotten from them is that they are orphans." I looked at Running-bear, witnessing his eyes shifting into a distant stare.

Then he slowly responded, "Orphan orbs are spirits who have forgotten how to be reborn; you need to create an energy ball and put the information they need into it. This ball will be a source of information like a library. When they come around, you can direct them towards the ball. Fill the ball with the message for them that they need to find a family that they like, wait for the family to create life, and then go into the baby and be born."

All of this was a bit overwhelming for me. Creating metaphysical libraries? But within two months, I was sitting in my bedroom by myself. I was in meditation, creating a ball of energy and filling it with all the information I thought a lost spirit would need to know about being born on this planet, including geographic advantages.

The workshop came to a close.

Now, Art Runningbear said to the class, "Meet once a week."

We set a time for Monday evenings after 6 p.m. yoga class. About ten of us showed up and practiced meditation and healing skills. Runningbear's guided meditations seemed to have a noticeable impact on slowing down my usually racing mind. Ideas and worries slowed down and became more organized and clarified. Some of the clearing and healing skills he had taught us would keep me very busy while I was sitting in the quiet room with the group. Most were way more experienced than me, so while they were looking inward, I was wandering all around the universe and different galaxies.

Throughout the next eighteen months, there was an advanced workshop, a timeline workshop, a healing drum construction workshop, and a drumming session. I also signed up for the one-on-one remote empowerment program with Art Runningbear, consisting of twenty one-hour sessions, using Skype videoconferencing. I would participate in two or three timelines with Runningbear guiding me, mostly traveling to other lifetimes during each session.

He had me describe what I was experiencing, and then he would always ask, "What did you learn in that lifetime?"

I saw a lot of interesting things during these timelines and experiences that looked like movies. I had my doubts about where these lifetime visions originated from, especially since I started to notice that in these past lives, I did a lot of things that I would never do in this lifetime. I also gained a new sense of confidence because even if I was making up every story I was experiencing, and even if they were not actually past lives at all, something was happening. I was seeing inside my imagination as I had never looked at it before.

During those eighteen months that I studied with this group, our weekly Monday night meetings filled me with skills, tools, new experiences, and answers. One evening, one of the gals brought in her new Oracle cards by Caroline Myss, life-purpose angel cards. We all sat in a circle on yoga mats, on Mexican blankets and bolsters. She instructed us to connect with our higher selves and angel guides and then pick one card out of the deck. I got excited as I watched the others choosing their cards. I felt so thankful to be right where I was. I felt so good. The first lady chose gardening and working with flower essence. Dianne and I smiled at each other. I was thinking, *that sounds good.* The next lady pulled the card "Family." She was really frustrated because she didn't want to have anything to do with her family at the moment, and she'd been complaining about family holiday problems.

The next girl said, "I don't know my angel guides."

I chimed in, "Me neither."

She picked "energy healer." I thought again, *that's for me, the energy healer.*

Then one of my favorite people in the group, Terry—the ex-cop from LA who read tarot cards from her mind's eye—pulled her card, "nutrition." The card described that she was going to heal people with her cooking.

She giggled and laughed. "I'm a cook? My husband's going to be glad to hear that."

I thought these cards had really nailed me again. Health through food was super important to me, another of my favorite subjects.

Dianne and I sat next to each other on the far side from the others as they flipped over their angel card, revealing their life purpose. We wiggled and giggled in delight because these were all things we loved and did well.

Then the cards were handed to me.

I said, "But they've already pulled all three of my cards."

Someone reassured me that those were back in the deck.

I took a deep breath, and I asked my angels to show me my path. I spread the deck in front of myself and quickly pulled one card from the messy pile.

"Oh, shit! It's just like I've been saying—I have so much more studying to do!" I was laughing.

"What card did you get?"

"Study."

I read my card: "Reading, research, education, to help you gain confidence and clarity about your career."

I was thinking, *I hope these angels don't expect me to actually go back to college.*

The description on my card said, "This card indicates that you will need additional information to feel confident about your career. Fortunately, the angels are guiding you clearly in this regard, so please notice recurring ideas and feelings about taking classes and about getting a mentor, reading a book or other forms of research and study."

I said, "I know; that's what I've been doing!" I was waving my arms around with excitement.

Dianne said, "That's what you've been doing! What a great validation!"

It was Dianne's turn to pull a card. She pulled "Write."

She said, "Oh no—writing?"

I had empathy for her. Because like me, she preferred baking, energy healing, and gardening. My card, "Study," mixed with my emotions toward school in my mind. I didn't do very well in school, and the very thought of more of it filled me with horror.

In ninth grade, my teacher had me removed from my elective drama class because I could not yet read out aloud, having difficulty pronouncing the words. I used to stutter as I confused the order of the words in the sentence, my mixed-up mind trying to make sense of what I was supposed to be saying. After my first mistake, my mind would go blank. I could hear my heartbeat grow louder and louder. Then I'd feel the heat of my face as it flushed from embarrassment.

San Diego County School District in the late seventies did not have the time, teacher power, or room in the overcrowded schools to assist students with unrecognized learning disabilities. Teachers and counselors just tried to keep me out of trouble. The teachers in the arts and crafts departments, however, enjoyed my creativity. During my senior year, I also actually received one grade of an A that wasn't from an art class. It was from a personal-development class, where I created a lecture on baking chocolate snapper cookies, modeled after Julia Child's TV cooking show. Somehow, I graduated from high school. Even though, I did not truly understand simple sentence structure and I had not even begun to understand the structure of a paragraph.

I remember a light bulb going off in my head in English 101 at a community college in San Diego, as I took the class for the third time. Make a statement, give support of the statement, and then close it with a summary. I told you what I said I would. And suddenly, there it was; I got an A in that class. I was thirty-four years old, and I had completed my first term paper. I'm sure there are plenty of teenagers who mastered those basic concepts of writing in high school. I had testing done at the community college, which showed that I had symbol problems. A learning disability, the counselor who tested me said; according to California state law, I was to be allowed as much time as I needed to complete testing.

The gift of time was all I really needed, and that led to this miraculous experience. During the final test for social anthropology, I was about ready to have a complete meltdown.

I recall thinking, *what letter does the word "the" start with?*

Forming my lips to make the sound of the TH, I thought hard.

Is it S? No, that's not it.

Oh, come on, I thought in frustration. Then I remembered something.

I had told the teacher not to limit my time on tests because I had a learning challenge. I realized I could sit there all day if I needed to, writing everything I'd learned in the last semester. I loved this class, and I hung on to the teacher's every word during the lectures.

It was the late nineties, and I had a Franklin speller, which only worked if you had the first letter of the word. If the first letter was a vowel, it could choose a different vowel than you had chosen to create your word. It really helped with correcting most of my jumbled messes of letters that I created when trying to spell a word. But a simple word like "the" without the capability of voice command as we have with today's technology was impossible. I drew letters on scrap paper, and finally I got it—and for the first time, I completed an essay test in my late thirties. In fact, I finished my test while other students were still working on theirs. As I left the room, I thought, *those poor kids! They're even slower than me.* Proudly, I can say I received the highest grade in that class on that final test.

But by now, I had lost interest in taking classes. Making money was easier and less time-consuming, and I was enjoying my life. It may have all been fear; what if I did make it through college? I think I was actually scared of getting a degree. I mean, what on earth would I do with it? Bosses expected employees to have more than basic writing skills, and most people had been using these skills since their teens. I felt I would never be able to have value as an employee in a professional position without polished writing skills.

Study—that angel life purpose card kept popping into my mind. My mind still programmed from society that study was traditional academics. Months went by, months in which I studied with that unusual group of healers. I did not realize how valuable all the things I was learning during those eighteen months would become. Some of the women in my group would complain the energy I brought was too strong and told me I needed to be gentler.

My always-supportive two best friends of the group were Dianne, also known to me as the powerful Princess, and Terry, who would describe amazing journeys she was experiencing through the eyes of an eagle. Once she told us a beautiful story a spirit guide had shown to her. She was climbing a huge mountain, and the dirt path wound around and around it. She struggled to reach the top of the mountain, and then the guide told her, you must bring others with you; it does no good to get to the top of the mountain without bringing the others along with you.

Well, these two special friends enjoyed my work, and they gave me full permission to practice on them anytime. I was practicing what I now know organizations like the Foundation of Shamanic Studies consider advanced techniques. I was extracting negative entities, doing distance energetic healing, clearing, journeying, and working with angels and spirit guides.

One day, I knew Terry would be very busy. She was leaving the next day to Alaska for a summer recreational vehicle fishing trip. Sometimes, she would complain about her back hurting. I went into meditation and performed a healing on her back. I texted her later that day and asked her how she was feeling. The first thing she replied was, she had been carrying around her grandbaby, and miraculously her back had not been bothering her. It always brought joy to my heart when my friends were feeling better than usual because I took the time to send body healings to them.

During our eighteen months of study, under the direction of Art Runningbear, my meditations and dreams held meaningful messages. My intuition climbed as my confidence grew, and my mind blossomed. We practiced as a group so many skills, including remote viewing, contract burning, reading each other's universes, healing conflicts in relationships, and hands-on healing. One time, I was spinning out from vertigo, and I texted how I was feeling to Kerry, the studio owner, and an active member of our group. Suddenly, everything stopped spinning. I was amazed.

I texted her again. "What did you do?"

She answered, "I grounded you."

Grounding was a tool we were taught the first day of class with Runningbear.

During the summer of 2013, I tried out a more advanced tool in Dianne's life that we had learned from Runningbear. She had told me she was having a hard time sleeping at night. Her dogs kept waking up during the night, growling and barking, and we had talked through all the possibilities. Maybe it was raccoons or coyotes. But she added she had seen a large black wing outside her living room window.

I wondered if it was a California condor; I had seen a pair of them flying over Carson Valley, and they were so much bigger than the turkey vultures and weren't flying in a circle.

I decided I would try something and see if I could have any impact on the situation. I went into meditation and did a timeline to take me to the moment when she had seen the wing. I was instantly next to a house, peering up at a winged monster with talons. The creature, surprised at my appearance, hissed and showed its fangs. It looked huge compared to me. Somehow, I had put myself there, and I was very small. But I didn't have any fear; I knew that energetic work could be done without any regard to time or space. That fact that I was the size of an orange-haired troll that I had carried around with me in my pocket in the seventies should have nothing to do with the effectiveness of my skills. My blonde hair was in warrior braids, and I was carrying my Star of David shield and sword. It makes me giggle that I suddenly appeared like a superhero while doing my spiritual warrior work.

I yelled up to that monster, "Hey, what are you doing looking in that window?"

"I'm watching the powerful princess," hissed the monster.

I was thinking, *no wonder she's disturbed by a creepy-looking thing like you; she is a powerful healer and bringer of light, and you resemble a demon.*

"It's none of your business what the princess is doing!" I yelled from my tiny body.

He snarled and huffed, "I will keep an eye on the princess if I want."

Then as he peered through the window into my friend's home, he asked, "What can you do to me, little girl?"

I acted humbly, and kindly asked for forgiveness for all mankind from this mystical-looking creature, and I added for it to leave and stay gone.

And then I smiled and looked him straight in the eyes and said, "This is what I can do!"

I demonstrated a fifth-dimension tool that Art Runningbear had taught us. I like to call this tool "flower power." It works because two identical things cannot fill the exact same space and time, or they will cease to exist. I created a large sunflower, then I created the same one next to it. Next, I imposed it over the first one, and they both vanished. He watched and without another threat, turned and bounded into the distance. I watched until he was gone.

Now, I admit I was feeling a bit proud of myself. Perhaps in the real world, my healings felt too strong for people. But in the metaphysical world, it felt like I was becoming a warrior. Yet I wasn't convinced that I had actually done anything that would change anything in the real world.

So, I texted Dianne. "Hey, I tried out something on the space around your place; let me know how you guys sleep tonight."

She texted back, "That is amazing. I'm grateful for all the insight and help. It's been really strange around here. My little dog hasn't slept all night in weeks."

I responded, "Well, I apologized for us to it and asked it to leave and stay gone. I did a flower power demo for it. Let me know if your dog does better tonight, and if not, I'll try again."

The next day, she texted, "Oh my goodness!! Whatever you did was very powerful! We all slept through the night! Nothing weird or intimidating happened. Thank you so much! You are the best. Love you a lot! Have an extra blessed day!"

I responded, "Oh, good."

Dianne texted back, "Yes, and thank you. You reminded me I've got tools to keep them away! When needed, forgiveness and flower power."

As the group formed by Runningbear worked together on Monday evenings, others of the group shared with us guided healing meditations, teaching us skills of protection, co-creating with nature spirits, and many other useful skills. My confidence as a healer and spiritual warrior grew. I studied, and I blossomed.

The experiences and the knowledge I gained during this time were immeasurable. I had always made jokes in my twenties that organized religion was much too new-fangled for me because it had only been around for a couple of thousand years. Perhaps it wasn't a joke, as I could feel the power of the ancient skills.

The reprimands that I received from the more advanced healers, that the energy I brought to the people was too strong, were confusing for me. My healings being too strong didn't make a bit of sense. I would think, *isn't it good to feel the energy? Don't people need the channels in their bodies cleared to make progress?* My two besties from the group, Dianne and Terry, were so supportive and encouraging. I kept practicing and studying.

In general, I enjoyed the diverse group, and I felt each of us had something special to offer. We took turns guiding the weekly meeting. Having no other meta-physical training behind me, I spent my turns as leader, reteaching skills from Runningbear. During my weekly private virtual sessions with Runningbear, I would ask him to review the skill I was planning on teaching; that way I could create clear notes to take to the Monday meeting. I was the most fascinated by the timeline skill. This is used to view and heal experiences that have already happened or that are going to happen in a soul's existence. We used this skill mostly to look at past lives and see what we learned from those lifetimes. Art Runningbear guided me through about twenty hours of these types of timelines. He called this the empowerment program.

Honestly, I can't say it was all fun. I was at times definitely feeling physically ill. After three past-life viewings within a single hour on videoconferencing, I would be literally spinning out in varying degrees from all the energy we had moved. This made me realize why people left metaphysical work to the leaders of organized religion or shamans. But I was feeling this work was the right path for me. Every session with Runningbear ended with *go outside, put your hand on a tree, and ground yourself*. I wondered if this would ever change, or would I always feel sick to my stomach and spinning out of my head from doing metaphysical work? Runningbear called the metaphysical changes that people went

SUSAN MARTIN

through during these empowering practices "the gross period." It certainly was a little rough, but I continued, and my conscious mind viewed deep subconscious thoughts during this six-month program. The ultimate result for me was that I'd become more present in this lifetime.

I experienced over sixty of these past life-viewings, and about three months into the empowerment program, I recall observing big changes in my personality. I was understanding why I was who I was and that I had chosen to be who I am. I also remember thinking, *I see why most people don't want to do this work.* It wasn't easy looking deep into my subconscious, seeing things that weren't very pretty or actually downright disgusting.

Timelines are performed like this: The facilitator guides the subject to a time in the past or future. This is something that you don't want to try without the guidance of a practitioner with advanced metaphysical training. The most important detail is that you give the subject clear starts and finishes to the needed timeline, so they don't get lost. This all gets a little abstract, but pieces of our souls can be in a lot of different places at the same time. In this human experience, it's best for us to have as much of our souls within our current bodies, creating a stronger being for the human experience. After years of metaphysical training, I have many skills and practices for assisting souls to be totally present in their own bodies.

One day, Runningbear started our private session with, "Let's look at the beginning and end of this life." This day, I got quite a surprise as I found myself about a hundred feet under the water with scuba gear on, but my air tank was suddenly empty. Something had happened; I assumed there had been a free flow from my scuba regulator. It was unclear exactly how this occurred, but at the point where I came into the event, I looked up, realizing I was very deep underwater with an empty air source.

My reaction was, "Really?"

I explained to Runningbear what I was seeing; it was my death—and it wasn't that far in the future.

He immediately said, "We are going to take that out of your timeline by simply clipping out the event like we're editing a film reel. Let's go back to just before the event."

I could see a long, flat dock surrounded by Caribbean water. We clipped out that experience, and he had me write a new death scene.

We finished up that day, and I could feel the immense energy we had moved; I was actually spinning out for days and had to reach out to a male friend for extra grounding. The mix of feminine and masculine energy grounds us as humans, and maybe that is why we are always looking for the opposite energy from other humans to bring us present. The perfect balance, the mix of yin and yang.

The craziness about this was when the financial adviser took me on a cruise in 2015. We were pulling into Cozumel, and I looked out the side of the cruise ship and saw the long, flat dock from that timeline. It was a bit creepy to participate in the two dives that day, and if that wasn't enough confirmation that the timeline of my life had been changed, I went back to Cozumel a few months later and dived six more dives. I also listened to Sean as he asked the divemaster about a really cool dive he had done in the past that brings you out of an underwater cave at 120 feet below the surface.

The divemaster explained to the financial adviser, "I don't think anyone wants to do that dive."

I thought to myself, *yeah, especially not me.*

The results of the Art Runningbear empowerment program were amazing. I came out of that program with a new sense of confidence, understanding the puzzle pieces it took to get me to this place in time. He had definitely created a new leaf on the timeline of my current life. The criticisms of the group toward me faded away, and now I was only hearing the praises.

A year after our group had ended, I invited Runningbear to my home. Dianne and Terry joined us for a review of the advanced timeline skill. I had a new assistant helping me around the house. I invited her to the meeting, and because she was my guest, I assigned her to be my partner for the review. She was trying the skill for the first time, and I was a bit surprised when, guided by her, I went to a lifetime as a mermaid. I saw a place that resembled Earth, but it felt different. It was like when you put a filter on a photo that makes it look like a painting. Everything on the Earth was there, but the colors were way more intense.

The beginning of life as a mermaid was also quite different; I saw the body created by a group. I call this group "the panel," and I had seen them in meditation a few times, seated in a large semicircle while I was standing in front of them on a stand, as they decided my fate. In these encounters, I can't see this group clearly, since they are always somewhat hidden in the dark. But in this timeline experience, I saw a mermaid body created by a few of them. They stood in robes with hands held out, and the body slowly grew out of thin air.

I thought, *Ah, so this is how mystical creatures are created.* Anyway, it seemed as if I lived as a mermaid for hundreds of years, and I remembered it being quite lonely.

When the group ended after eighteen months of study, I was thirsty for more metaphysical lessons and found Jeffery Allen with Mind Valley, an online school. His Duality course was a weekly meeting for two months, and it helped me to understand the work I was already practicing. I enjoyed the worldwide meditations and healing energy work.

He talked about fairies being spirit guides. I hadn't understood that when I did 108 days of meditation in a row months before. During a meditation, I'd gotten a little aggressive with a negative energy and not followed respectable protocol. The panel assigned me thirty days of community service of spending time while I was in meditation with the fairies, and this experience was delightful.

Some highlights I recall. I taught a group to ballroom dance, and we dressed up and went to a wedding in a castle, and we all danced. They also showed me that little white flowers should be added to honey and used as medicine for people. There were baby fairies all the way to the old, grumpy witch fairy who tried to scare us. I felt like a fairy queen as I worked within my imagination for thirty days in a row during my meditations. One day, I brought them an ice-cream maker and made them ice cream in the magical forest. I didn't understand I was doing journeys; I just was having fun in my imagination, and I'm so lucky all these things come so naturally to me.

After this, I moved in with Sean the financial adviser. I also took more private yoga lessons, but this time from Dianne's lovely daughter Taylor. These yoga lessons prepared me for my trip to India for two-hundred-hour yoga training. I ended the year traveling to the Indian spiritual capital and the birthplace of yoga, Rishikesh, located at the base of the Himalayas. I had found this school simply by searching on the internet; the course could be completed in just thirty days, and its cost was less expensive than any similar school in the world. I had grown up in Southern California, traveling to Mexico with my parents and friends, so thankfully I knew how to eat, drink, and behave in risky environments.

The most shocking thing to me during my travels to India was the piles and piles of trash. Trash is generally burned in India, and trash piles with plastics emit toxic fumes. The streets of the neighborhood, for a few hours of the day, would be heavy with the stench of burning trash.

We are all so spoiled in the United States, where trash seemingly magically disappears weekly, taken away by organized trash companies. Despite all the trash in India, however, my travel to the northern Ganges

River was amazing. People came to Rishikesh to ride the rapids, to visit ashrams, to drink the river water for purification, and to visit the many holy temples.

The brightly colored temple buildings contrasting against the aqua-colored river are mind-blowingly beautiful. The weather in late November/early December was a tranquil seventy-five degrees. Tired-looking, underweight cattle chewed vegetarian scraps on street corners. Most yards contained one or two hungry-looking brahma bulls.

Interestingly, these communities still used the livestock to farm, and it felt like stepping back in time; it was all so serene and beautiful. I especially enjoyed watching the neighbors preparing their field and throwing handfuls of seeds onto the dirt to grow their rice. It was quite an experience to sit and watch in real time the planting of crops by hand, just as it had been done for thousands of years.

My memories of Rishikesh are of monkeys stealing balls of flour intended for the huge carp waiting in the majestic Ganges near the walkway to the Lakshman Jhula suspension bridge, bright-colored silken scarves filling shop windows, yummy baked goods, and the intoxicating resin logs of sandalwood burning in the street markets. There is also still clear in my thoughts, the town's hills crowded with ashrams for the study of yoga and meditation. The market streets filled with the brightly clothed wealthy tourists from the south of the continent who flock to the holy capital with huge smiles as they enjoy the wonders of the holy city. There was also the most memorable man with no legs or arms sitting on a blanket on the side of the street, collecting coins and bills. He smiled at me with the most honest joy, as I gifted him a few rupees. I'm not sure where I learned my greatest lessons, in the classroom of the ashram or on the streets of Rishikesh.

After I returned from India, I completed my three-hundred-hour yoga-teacher training with Angie and started an afterschool yoga program through Make a Real Difference Foundation. I had been working with MRD since 2010, the connection having started when I got the one-word message "orphans" from the orbs. Olivia Tearnan, the executive director of Make a Real Difference, was the only person I knew who did anything for orphans. I had been to a few of her toy-drive parties, at which she always had said she was collecting toys for the orphans.

I started helping with her fundraisers in 2010, but by 2018, I was teaching gentle yoga classes for adults and had started an afterschool yoga class for an elementary school once a week.

Olivia always seemed to magically connect everyone with whomever they needed to be connected to, and she humbly did—and does—so much for the community. She even introduced me to my Reiki Master, Michael.

I'm so grateful to so many people who knowingly or unknowingly assisted me on my journey to become a warrior.

CHAPTER 3

The Channel

Kaylee asked, "Are we going to get spa treatments in Sedona?"

I thought, *what, overpriced tourist massages?* I answered my friend, "No"

She asked, "So, what are we going to do?"

I answered, "I don't really know."

I was thinking we were going there for travel experience and hopefully to do some healing work.

As Sedona was known for its energy vortexes, I was interested in exploring the area and feeling what it would be like to do healing work there. I was also wondering if maybe next year I could get a job at a high-end spa, perhaps working in reception, or maybe even doing healings. In fact, I'd already been checking the internet for schools and workshops in the Sedona area. As Kaylee and I chatted, I tried to picture myself standing outside some upscale spa with a handwritten sign saying FREE HEALING. I wondered, *how is that going to work?*

We had planned this trip for the last three months, and it seemed a bit surreal that it was finally here. I had made the arrangements to fly to Sedona with Kaylee early in the morning on my birthday. Originally my thoughts were, this way I wouldn't be moping about alone as I turned another year older. But now that it was time to go to the spiritual capital of the United States, I was truly excited.

We landed in Phoenix, Arizona, where I changed in the restroom of the car-rental place, getting out of my heavy sweats and tennies into a knit cotton dress and sandals. I had gotten warm, and it felt good to change into lighter-weight clothes. The desert area of Phoenix was still warm, although it was technically winter in North America. But the air had been chilly when our flight took off that late-November morning and I'd worn several layers of clothes to keep warm on the flight.

I drove the rented sedan to Sedona; it was early afternoon now, and the two-hour-plus drive was getting long, so I was feeling sleepy. As we entered the city, we saw a handwritten sign on the road: PSYCHIC SHOW. We looked at each other and made a quick decision to turn in.

Seven dollars each just to enter this thing? I thought, as we stood at the front door peering into the conference room, both trying to get a read on the value of attending. I looked in and saw a strange-looking thin, tall lady with a frizzy red hair and one large geode-type rock on her table.

It was not that this was the only rock on the table; it was just the only one I really saw.

It looked intriguing enough, and so—still a little reluctantly—I paid the entrance fee, and we started to walk around the hotel conference room lined with tables. There was a person offering a photo of your aura with a reading of it. I have always found these photos interesting, with a picture that shows the colors around your body, reds, blues, yellows. I'm not sure if the reading would've been a psychic reading or just a reading of the physical colors. There were also assorted brightly colored crystals for sale, plus interesting jewelry and strange pendants giving off a creepy vibe. Kaylee purchased a crystal that she resonated with, and I bought a liquid supplement made with gold.

We slowly made it back to the front of the room, to the lady and the rock. The lady had synthetic-looking hair that seemed to be originating from the southwestern-style black felt hat she wore. Her clothes looked expensive and well made, a black jacket with large lapels lined with rivets, a long black layered skirt, and a wide leather-fringed belt with lots of metal details. The strange thing was that her clothes were clearly unwashed, and her toenails that were revealed by the worn sandals looked unkempt. I found myself wondering, *does she have a home?*

I examined the rock. Its rough dark-gray exterior contrasted its snow-white and light-peach crystal tunnel interior. The rock itself was big, about ten inches wide and six inches high. I held my hands one each side of the open ends. The vibration that emanated from it was very intense. I was thinking, how did she charge this rock up to that high of a vibration? I'm not that sensitive, and yet I can really feel it.

Kaylee put her hands near the openings of the rock, and she explained she felt a cool wind. Now, things were getting even stranger. I felt baffled as to why she didn't feel the same thing as me. Art Runningbear had taught me to infuse energy into rocks, but I had never felt any rock give off this kind of vibration, so I was amazed and full of wonder.

"How much for this?" I asked.

"One hundred and eighty dollars. It's a geode of apophyllite crystal. I can just imagine that there is a fairy living inside," the tall, thin lady answered.

I looked into the open end of the small tunnel on the rock, hoping to see a tiny-winged creature. The interior was a forest of sparkling crystals, but I didn't see anything alive in it.

The thin lady with red hair began telling us her story. She had been a channel since she was six years old, and she told us that she'd had a series of near-death experiences during infancy that she was sure had caused her to have these abilities. She answered a couple of questions we had about ourselves with no charge and made a few insightful comments with regard to me. Then I moved the conversation to focus on Kaylee.

I asked, "I'm wondering what my friend should be focusing on for a career?"

She told us Kaylee had a rare ability to hear animals' thoughts.

Kaylee confirmed this with a story about her family fish's thoughts earlier that morning.

We were both asking plenty of questions and enjoying ourselves.

"How about you gals meet me tomorrow for lunch, and I give you a lesson on channeling?" the lady offered, suddenly taking us both by surprise.

We both chimed in, "Okay!"

And it was a done deal; we would never turn down the chance to learn something new. We made it back to our car, eager to find our hotel, and we giggled and chatted about our experiences so far.

Finally, we arrived at our hotel, which was a bit out of town and heading into the mountains. The lodge sat surrounded by pine trees and was at least fifteen degrees cooler than it had been in the lower part of the city of

Sedona. Our room was wonderful, with a huge rock fireplace. We changed quickly and headed back into town for my birthday dinner. I chose nachos, intent on celebrating. The evening passed in a blur of laughter and contentment, as we were both very relaxed but excited about our unfolding adventure.

We returned to our room, and I built a big birthday fire in the massive rock fireplace. At this point, I was feeling very pleased with my life and choices. Because of working the night before and going straight to the airport, I had already been awake for thirty-one hours. We got to bed early and slept well.

The channel had told us about the airport vortex, and she had suggested we go there in the morning. She added something about the fact that we would know when we were at the vortex by the way all the trees grew in spirals. So, we walked into the park and followed the trail the ranger at the entry booth had sent us on. We were enjoying the views, chatting, and then suddenly noticed how the trees had become very twisted.

We stopped and were taking pictures. Kaylee sat down near a twisted tree and went off into a meditation. I wandered away and then struck up a conversation with a man whose wife was nearby.

The man said, "This is the third place we have been like this. We heard it's supposed to be some sort of energy center. But I don't feel anything."

I asked, "Are the places you are talking about the vortexes?"

The man said, "Yes, I think that's what they called them … vortexes."

I said, "To me, this vortex feels extremely clear, but I haven't been to any of the others. I work with energy. Would you like to try out some energy work? Maybe then you will feel something."

The man said with a quick response, "Yeah, sure."

I called across to his wife. "I'm going to put my hands on your husband's shoulders and give him a hands-on energy healing."

She was standing about twenty feet away and chatting with Kaylee. She smiled and nodded.

Then, I motioned for the man to sit down on the hillside. I squatted behind him and placed my hands on his shoulders. The energy around me felt very light, and I felt very supported by the area. *I could do this for twelve hours a day here, it feels so airy!* I thought.

Only a few moments had passed, and his wife was moving in closer to us and staring at the healing going on. Using my mind, I quickly cleared his first and second chakras. My thoughts brought my attention to his wife, as I sensed that the blocks I was seeing were hers and not his.

I asked the wife, "Would you like a healing also?"

She nodded, and we shuffled around, so I now had my hands on her shoulders. I also cleared her first and second energy centers, starting from the base of her spine. We all have seven chakras running the length of our bodies, and I sometimes see these centers in people looking gray or foggy. I let cosmic energy flow through her chakras only for a few minutes. Everything then felt and looked clear, and the whole session was probably done in less than twenty minutes. We all chatted together, and we learned they were from Tennessee. They told me they had never met anyone like me before.

The man said, "No one like you lives in Tennessee!"

I answered, "Well, I don't live here in Sedona either.

We came here for my birthday. Thank you for letting me do the healing. It was a goal. I wanted to feel how it would be to work here, in this spot."

I smiled to myself, pleased I had done the free healing I had been imagining.

Having said goodbye to the couple, Kaylee and I walked away to the top of the nearby hill. We had noticed there were a lot of people gathered there, and now we realized this was the actual airport vortex.

Kaylee said, "That couple looked like two completely different people before and after you worked on them. That was amazing!"

"Thank you! Well, I just hope they feel better than they did before I gave them the healing. It was effortless to work at that vortex."

Then we enjoyed ourselves like teenagers, clicking selfies and posting them on social media.

We headed to lunch at the Indian restaurant where we were supposed to meet up with the channel. Our bellies were rumbling; we had delayed eating without her for more than an hour already when the restaurant phone rang. The Indian man answered and then looked over my way and brought the land line phone to our table. I felt like a mob boss in the seventies as I put the receiver to my ear and said, "Hello?" Kaylee was deeply amused too; having only been born in 1989, she had never known anything but cell phones for restaurant calls. She giggled.

We were done eating by the time the lady wearing the same clothes as yesterday arrived. The call had explained she had been tied up with some legal stuff and that we should get started with our food, especially as I said we were really hungry and the food smelled so good.

She ate her lunch. Then we got into the rental car and headed off to Boynton Canyon. As we were getting out of the car, this story gets a little crazy.

The channel said, "One night, I was working in my metaphysical shop, and a couple came in. Their clothes were all dusty, and their faces were pale. They told me that someone had sent them to me to get a healing. They had been out in Boynton Canyon after sunset, and an invisible force had pushed them down into the dirt trail."

As we walked toward the trailhead, she added, "You know, because of that, I never stay out here after dark. This canyon is cursed by four Indian nations."

I was thinking, *so why are we coming here for class? The energy doesn't feel clear and light like the airport vortex. It feels heavy and thick.* I also think, *luckily, it's only two thirty in the afternoon, so we have lots of time before it gets dark.*

The channel walked very slowly, and we stopped before we hit the trailhead.

Then she said, "Put your hands out."

She demonstrated to us by holding her hand away from her side with her palm facing down toward the earth. We mimicked her, and I could feel a vibration coming up from the dirt.

Kaylee said, "I can feel it."

I added, "Me too."

We walked down the dirt trail, the channel wobbling, slipping, and tripping on the very rocky path. Her sandals offered none of the support needed by her bony feet, and I was worried she was going to fall down. So, I offered my arm for support, and together we all made our way down the dusty trail, watching out for loose crumbles of granite that could cause us to slip and fall. Soon, we came to a bench.

There, the channel said, "Sit down. We are going to ask permission to work."

She added a story of how one time at Pyramid Lake, Nevada, she didn't ask permission to do some metaphysical work and had ended up in a terrible windstorm, hiding under her truck. Well, I could believe that, as I was familiar with Pyramid Lake, a tribal burial site and final resting place of some very unfortunate Chinese railroad-track laborers. This massive lake sits in the middle of the high desert on a Paiute reservation. Storms can whip up pretty fast in this type of terrain. I took a mental note never to set to work without asking for permission on any tribal land.

I went into silent prayer and asked, "May I have permission to work?"

I got back, "No."

I asked again and got another "No."

I rephrased my question this third time. "I humbly ask if I may have permission to work."

I received a clear knowing of "Yes."

We walked about a mile down into the canyon, and the only life we had seen was one mountain biker and three young deer. We finally got to a location the channel was satisfied with, and I found one smooth, flat rock to use as a seat. Kaylee sat just to my right, and the channel stayed standing in front of us in the middle of the narrow, dusty trail. The winter brush surrounded our makeshift classroom.

The channel said, "We are working with universal mind."

She was channeling about us, telling us telling us where our souls were formed. My home, she said, was Arcturus. She described me as being surrounded by a rainbow and told me to work with Hilarion as a guide, and with the Rainbow Healers of light for healing work.

The air by now was starting to chill. It was getting late, and I was getting antsy. The canyon was creepy, and I wanted to get out of there before it was dark, especially after what she had told us about the odd occurrence with the couple. I shifted about on my rock seat uneasily. She kept channeling away and talking and talking.

Finally, it was evident that she too began to get cold, and she eventually responded to my third rather obvious hint that it was now time to go. We started back to the trailhead and parking lot. Now, she was really slow and wobbly, and Kaylee had one arm and I the other. I was silently saying a mantra of gratitude in my mind the whole way out of the canyon.

"Thank you so much for letting us work here today. Please let us leave safely."

In my imagination, I saw a black wolf on the trail about fifteen feet in front of us. It was getting really dusky and cold by the time we passed the bench where we had asked permission to work earlier in bright sunlight; now it was almost completely dark. When we reached the parking lot, it was an eerie pitch black that enveloped us.

I felt relief washing over me as we returned safely to the car, and I said, "We made it, and in my imagination, I only saw one black wolf crouched on the trail, snarling at us."

The channel said, "It had to be a black wolf?"

I chuckled, feeling amused that she was complaining about the "degree of scariness" in my imagination, after she was the one who had kept us out there so late. I gave one more prayer of gratitude as we left the canyon unharmed. We were cold and sleepy, and as of yet, we had not been taught to channel.

We all decided it was time for a coffee break. I googled, and I found a grocery store, as I got out of the car, the channel asked me to get her a Milky Way candy bar. This made me giggle inside. The channel wants a candy bar named after a galaxy.

I also ordered us some coffees at the in-store Starbucks and managed to find notebooks for Kaylee and me to use for taking notes. We had already filled our one small notepad during the afternoon class out at the canyon.

The coffees warmed us and slowly woke up our brains. The channel then told us some crazy story of a client who had wanted her to perform a marriage of this client to Archangel Michael. The wedding had been planned, complete with witnesses, cake, and flowers. It had all gone quite awry as vendors noticed it was just a fantasy wedding. It proved to be a very funny story, and we were entertained.

But all the while, I felt as if she really wasn't getting how much talent Kaylee and I had, and that she had been kind of talking down to us. I ask her to channel a question of where the healing energy I'd been working with came from. She channeled and then came back quickly.

She said, "Godhead; that's impressive." She then channeled and gave me specific instructions to perform a healing on Kaylee's boyfriend. The instructions were clear to use the Rainbow Healers of Light for very short periods of time and to direct the energy to very specific areas of his neck and head. I took exact notes, understanding that these were important instructions.

I also asked, "Can you please channel if it's okay for me to do plant medicine in December in Costa Rica, with my mentor that lives there?"

She answered, "They say *no*; they showed me that you would be in a gray column. You would lose abilities."

I took this information and canceled my planned trip to Costa Rica.

Then there were more stories from her, and finally, around 11:00 p.m., she at last, gave us a mantra of protection and the technique to channel. It was a bit of a trippy experience for me. In my imagination, as I practiced the new skill, I saw a large man in robes with a thin, kind face. The instructions from the channel were, after safely transporting ourselves to a faraway place beyond universes, to find and merge with our chosen spirit guide. In my mind's eye, I saw that when I started toward Hilarion, the feeling of his energy was so intense that I backed away. I tried again and again, but it was just as strong these times too, so I shied away again and again. I was gliding in and out, around, and back in, and then finally, I got up the courage to merge with the spirit guide and ask my question.

Earlier in the night, the channel had said she might be able to channel our spirit names, and now that we had finally gotten our lesson, we asked her to try. She attempted to channel Kaylee's spirit name first and came back with an unclear message. But then she channeled my spirit name and came right back, then said with complete certainty, "Rainbow Dancer."

As soon as she announced this, Kaylee and I chuckled. I repeated the new title.

The channel then explained, "They said you looked like a rainbow, and you were dancing around like a figure eight up there."

She had told me earlier that I had a complete rainbow crown chakra, and I wondered how I'd got that. Maybe it was those clearing meditations Running-bear had taught me. Or maybe I'd been born with it.

I drove us back to the channel's beat-up van, still parked outside the Indian restaurant, and we were chatting when suddenly Kaylee shuffled around in the back seat. The channel and I both turned to look at her. She was sitting facing toward us as if nothing had happened.

I asked, "Are you okay?"

She answered, "Yeah."

We negotiated a fee for the day, including the rock. The channel had taken the time to channel about why I should own this rock, and she told me this apophyllite elevated my consciousness. I thought it was a really cool rock, and I paid for it. But I was also thinking, *Really? I had to buy a twelve-pound rock?* How was I going to get this through airport security?

The channel had cleverly lightened her load of one large geode, and we paid her a fair price for the long thirteen-hour day. We decided that it was a lot of entertainment and a very nice rock for a total of five hundred dollars, and we were very happy with our new skill.

We drove back to the hotel.

Kaylee turned to me during the drive and said, "This Indian guy in full buckskin with fringes down the sleeves, and holding up a tomahawk, was running at the car. It scared the shit out of me. I thought he was real, but he disappeared instead of hitting the car, and I realized he was just a spirit."

I was pretty amazed. "Just a spirit?'

No wonder she had been shuffling about in the back seat! If I'd seen a spirit running at the car, there would be no way I could have just sat there as if nothing had happened. *Man, this chick is badass!* I thought.

She also confirmed she had seen a black wolf and an Indian with no shirt standing by the side of the trail; his arms were crossed, and he had been staring at us with an unhappy glare as we had exited the canyon. My dreams of living in this area were quickly diminishing, since I really didn't want to live among a bunch of unhappy Native American spirits. That just sounded very unreasonable. By the time we got back to our room, it was close to 2:30 a.m.

I said, "Where are we, Vegas? What are they pumping into the air around here?"

I was totally amazed that we had hardly slept and had stayed up half the night, I noticed Kaylee was looking a little stressed.

I asked, "Are you okay?"

She answered, "I feel like there are all these angry spirits coming at me."

I created protection, forming a large pyramid above us and a large, inverted pyramid below us, and then I brought the bottom one up and the top one down, so it looked like a three-dimensional Star of David, and I spun the star, a trillion times a second. Kaylee looked instantly relaxed.

Curious, I asked her, "What happened when I did that?"

She answered, "Everything went blank."

I taught her the skill. Then we went to bed and both slept soundly.

I woke up at 6:00 a.m. and said, "Let's go back to that coffee shop we found yesterday; I want more of that quiche. I haven't stopped thinking about it since."

Kaylee said, "That sounds so yummy!"

As we dressed, we chatted about yesterday's adventure.

"Do you think that lady was all human?" I asked, deep in thought. "She kind of looked like an alien."

Kaylee answered, "She said she was a walk-in."

"A walk-in? What is that?"

"When one soul leaves and another takes over the body."

"Oh yeah, I did that one lifetime. I saw this experience during a past lifetime timeline with Art Runningbear. I came out of a veil of black I'd been exiled to during caveman times by a visible God in the sky. I entered into the bright world of earth, and the blue, the green … I was marveling at all the color after millions of years of blank darkness, and I saw a family down on the beach near a dock where a large ship was moored."

I kept explaining to Kaylee, "There was a baby on the beach amongst a family. I swooped down and entered the body the other soul had decided they were ready to get out; it felt it had made a bad choice and did not want to live the life of a slave trader's son."

Kaylee said, "Hmm, I think she's probably only part alien."

I came back with, "Ugh, those aliens! Hopefully, it's for the good of mankind some of them don't seem so nice. Well, at least we know my spirit name now! Rainbow Dancer!"

We giggled.

Kaylee said, "I was feeling it was a little sketchy yesterday as she led us into a deserted, cursed canyon."

I laughed. "I know! I was totally creeped out!"

Kaylee continued, "I was thinking, have we made a mistake? Are we in danger? But I do think it's cool she teaches levitation. I would love to learn how do that."

Yesterday, I had pictured her standing in front of a typical group of metaphysical devotees. Some unshaven man, one man just a little too pretty, and assorted shapes and sizes of middle-aged women. I was thinking that to get to see even one of them float above the ground would have been well worth the fee for the class.

I asked, "I wonder if anyone actually did it?"

We headed back home with our new skill. The next day, we practiced.

"Ask what the whale song means?" Kaylee texted.

I channeled and got a clear answer: "LOVE."

CHAPTER 4

The Sweats in San Diego

Native American Sweat Lodge

I was very grateful to be invited to participate in the beautiful Native American prayer ceremony Inipi. I was also very grateful to the chief for inviting me back, no matter how many faux pas I happened to commit. These Inipis were guided by him, a medicine man, and held in a lodge created with blankets, laid over willow sticks that had been woven to create a half-dome-shaped low hut.

In the center of the hut, a shallow pit was dug into the earth. This was the space where stones taken from the nearby sacred fire would be carefully placed by the

SUSAN MARTIN

medicine man, then sacred sage water added, producing a very hot steam that filled the hut with a rapid burst of heat.

We sat circled around the steaming rocks, singing and praying to Grandfathers, Father Sky, and Mother Earth. On this day, there were three separate ceremonies. The first one was all women, and I was very honored to attend. This sweat was very special, as we had with us two women who were pregnant. Next, there was an all-men's sweat and then a group sweat.

After we completed the sweats, we all enjoyed food that we had brought in potluck style. Then we smoked a prayer pipe. We were warned not to inhale and shown how to properly hold it, then instructed on how to— with intention—direct the smoke to the heavens to Father Sky, toward the ground to Mother Earth, then to our left and right, saluting the four directions. Sweats, refreshments, and the pipe-smoking ceremony were complete.

Some people had already left the gathering, but about fourteen of us were still seated in a circle on chairs and wooden benches on the patio of the yard. The yard

114

contained the sacred fire to heat the ceremonial rocks, a few large bushes that provided the sage for the sacred water, and the dome-shaped hut.

The medicine man was seated directly to my right, and now he got up, faced me, shook my hand, and thanked me for coming. As he moved to the person immediately to my left, a young man close by told me to get up and follow him and do the same. I did. It wasn't until I had completed the entire circle of guests, shaking their hands and thanking them for attending, that I became aware that no one else had done the same thing as me.

The single word out of my mouth was a whispered "Shit!" as I returned to my seat and realized what had happened! Then I gave a long, hard stare at the kid who had sent me on my journey around the patio. It must have been quite descriptive, because he apologized immediately. All of this caused such a ruckus that the chief had hushed us and reminded us that the Great Father was present. I was really embarrassed.

I thought I'd never be invited back. But I was, and now here I am, seated tall on blanket-covered earth with my feet crossed and tucked into my groin. My body was covered in a long, black cotton skirt, wet with sweat and water.

I'd had a strong and steady asana practice since 2012. I'm not saying I'd done yoga every day, but I'd done a lot, and now, seated for the fifth time of the day in an Inipi, I was thankful for my strength and flexibility.

The first four traditional doors had been held by the chief. His talks had been inspiring, and he explained we were allowed to travel anywhere we wanted to journey. With my breath, I let the warmth enter my body. The heat woke up my inner spirit. The external experiences of my life melted away. I felt I was in the womb of the earth. In my mind's eye, I sat in an open meadow near a flowing stream.

The chief called for the fire men to bring in more hot rocks. He called out, "Bring the Stone People."

I felt this meant he was recognizing the rocks as live spirits, another example of how everything here on earth is alive and here to support us. There were a lot of prayers, but the most memorable one for me was the praying for the next seven generations to be able to still practice prayer as we were doing today. The right to pray that thought touched my heart; may those rights never be taken away from anyone.

The four doors of the Inipi each represented a different direction of the four ages described by the sacred White Buffalo Calf Women; west, north, east, and south, or bear, buffalo, eagle, and coyote. There were stories and prayer songs for each door. The hut entrance was made of blankets that were folded back in between each session, letting in air and light.

Then more Stone People were added to the round circle cut into the earth. I lost count of the hot rocks that were pulled in from the sacred fire and carefully brushed off by the fire men, then placed within the tent for the medicine man to add to the pit. The stones piled up in the shallow dirt pit in the middle of the white willow-branched hut. We placed bits of cedar out of red pouches onto the rocks, with prayers. The smell from the burning sweet cedar swirled into the air, and sacred white sage water was added by the medicine man. As it made contact with the Stone People, hot steam billowed off the rocks, instantly raising the temperature to somewhere between hot and hotter.

The blankets were then folded back down, carefully sealing off all the light and containing the heat and steam. Drumming would start next, then song, and our bodies were filled with vibrations from the heady beat and the rapturous singing. If I'd had my eyes open or closed, I would have seen the same thing. There was no light from the outside, and I tried to physically look at what I was seeing in the darkness and decided to relax and see where spirit would take me. At one point, I was a warrior running through the tunnels that wound through the earth. Another time, I was devoured by an unknown beast. None of this was new to me; this is how I traveled and healed my soul with journey in the past. Today I was enjoying the journey. I was not asking questions of the spirit world. I was simply looking for the strength to enjoy my life. The fourth door was then completed, and the blankets were folded back.

"When you leave the lodge going from dark to light, it represents the liberation from the physical universe. All that is impure is left in the sweat lodge."

—AKTA LAKOTA MUSEUM & CULTURAL CENTER

We exited the lodge into the much cooler air, and we ate a bite of the sacred food that the women had prepared, representing the four directions. As we stood in a circle around the sacred fire in the center of the yard, we offered a pinch of tobacco from a pouch. With the dried leaf tobacco in our right fists, we gestured toward Father Sky and the four directions, and touched Mother Earth. Next, we each threw the prayer-filled leaf into the fire.

Ceremony completed, I shook the chief's hand, and he asked me if I was going to attend the second sweat. But I'd lost track of time in the first sweat and knew I had plans at 7:00 p.m.

I ignorantly asked, "What time is it?"

He teased, "A stick past a rock and a stone."

I took the teasing well. I had just asked the time from a man I'd witnessed leading a sacred ceremony. I chuckled to myself. I enjoyed the fact that I was so comfortable with the chief. He was so available and present for his family, and he called me *niece* throughout the day, and during ceremony many times with a special loving tone—one I'd only noticed before in my mother's or sister's voices.

I really had enjoyed watching the chief perform blessings during the sweat with a pair of eagle wings that he kept tucked above his head in the white willow branches that made the frame of the lodge. Watching him work was a magical experience. He tapped the eagle wings on the participant's head or brushed the feathers down their shoulders, backs, and arms, as he blessed each attendee.

We had each also tucked something into the willow branches, a small prayer bundle made from tobacco-stuffed fabric tied to look like a spirit, to carry our prayers to the Creator.

I felt blessed to witness this ceremony, and I loved that today while we were in the lodge, we had smoked the sacred prayer pipe. I like smoking the prayer pipe; I liked sucking the smoke into my mouth then picking the proper direction for blowing the smoke out through my pursed lips. Tasting the sweet leaf as it flowed over my tongue.

Then I joined the second sweat. There were only three women, one first-timer male, the two fire men, and the helper. The helper was leading, and with all the open real estate, I sat cross-legged, close to the hot rocks, and placed my hands on my knees. I didn't hide my face in my lap but let the steam hit it. I also discovered a new sensation: if I blew hot air out of my mouth at my hands and arms, it felt burning hot! I was in wonder, not knowing why the breaths felt like fire when they hit my skin.

In the dark with the hot steam, I felt very safe.

The first door ended, and one man asked to exit when the fire man jumped up to gather more Stone People.

He asked, "Permission to leave?"

There was no answer.

He asked again, "May I leave?"

The helper slowly shook his head no.

I smiled to myself. This big warrior man wearing a black kilt, as he helped the other men prepare the yard for ceremony, was trying to ditch out on the last few minutes of Inipi?

He asked one more time. The apprentice noncha-
lantly shook his head no, while he shifted around,
preparing for the next door. This time, I patted the
blanket-covered ground between us, and the kilt-wearing warrior of a man looked my way.

I said, "You can do this. It's going to be easy, just
one more."

The helper softly added, "Last door."

That was what it took, and he relaxed back down
into a seated position. His breath was not relaxed,
however, but it hadn't been for the past four doors
either. I breathed slow, calm breaths, hoping his spirit
could feel the ease and calm itself too.

The drumming was loud now, and it was dark, so
no one could see me. I played my air drum, keeping
the tempo with the helper. I was glad no one else could
see me showing off enjoying the heat and adding the
vigorous hand motions of drumming. I smiled to
myself; this felt like I was experiencing the fire circle
with my friends I would often see in journey.

We were eating the food, celebrating our completed
ceremony, the young fire man to my right and the black

kilt-wearing-warrior to my left. The kilt-wearing man said he was so thankful he didn't leave early, as he would have punished himself excessively if he'd cut out. He mentioned something about having PTSD.

I talked to him about this. "It must feel really good to succeed through an uncomfortable situation, realizing you were ill at ease but you were safe."

The two traditional sweats with the chief had never seemed excessively hot to me. My first sweat in this yard was a women's only, with two pregnant ladies in attendance. It seemed mild. But I confess, I'd felt very uncomfortable in a nonnative run sweat in the past. I found the fire man smirking as I told the story of my first sweat, where I had my face pressed into the dirt and gravel so I could position my mouth next to the bottom edge of the hut. This way I could breathe the slightest leakage of cool air from outside.

I was still curious about the black-kilt-wearing man.

I turned to him and asked, "So, what is your spiritual practice?"

He said, "I was a Zen monk for a short stint. But I quickly realized it wasn't my path."

I was amazed. "How long were you a Zen monk?"

He answered, "I didn't make it very long. I began in April, and I'd quit by September."

I calculated that to be five months in the monastery. That sounded like an eternity to me.

He added, "I had a really strong practice before I entered, so I thought I could do it, but the master would tell you to sit and count your breaths. I would ask for how long. He would only say, 'I'll tell you when you're done.' The only thing was, he would never return, and I was just left there alone with my thoughts."

I laughed. Good thing we managed to keep him in the hut for those last few minutes, a very easy task compared to seemingly endless hours of meditation at a monastery. I believed I was a spiritual neophyte in comparison to this guy, and I marveled at the fact he was so humble.

He sparked my interest in saying, "I was just left there alone with my own thoughts." My mind examined his statement; those hideous recordings in my head, continuously hitting the replay button, could be quite taxing.

CHAPTER 5

Cairns

There were a few more card readings over the phone while I was in San Diego.

Kaylee said, "They are saying Croatia."

"Cool! Croatia sounds like fun."

Kaylee exasperatedly said, "They're getting mad at me. I'm not understanding them. They're telling me they're not saying 'Croatia.' They're saying you need to go to a place in Australia."

"Australia is a big place. Can we narrow it down a little?"

I sent her a map. I asked her to go through the cities and ask the guide yes or no.

Kaylee said, "They are saying you need to go to

Cairns. There is an imbalance. A healing that needs to be done by you."

Then she got the word she was misunderstanding and exclaimed, "He's saying he's from Crow Nation!"

"Am I supposed to go to Crow Nation?" I asked.

Kaylee replied, "He says you can go to Crow Nation if you want, but you've already been given the message."

I looked up Cairns, "the gateway to the Great Barrier Reef."

I shared with Kaylee, "I'll do that. I'll buy the plane ticket to go do metaphysical charity work there. That sounds like a great trip!"

The day of travel arrived quickly, and San Diego to Los Angeles was an easy flight; it all turned out to be very leisurely. I made small talk with fellow travelers as I ate my dinner, determined to keep involved with persons in my surroundings, staying open to others who may have access to some knowledge that I needed for my journey. There was healing to be done, and at this point, I wasn't sure if it was for me or Cairns.

I headed down to the international flight terminal. Soon, I was struggling to unclasp the front chest strap of my backpack, wanting to organize my belongings, ideally to a duffel carry-on to make things easier. I struggled and struggled, but the clasp just wouldn't come open. I had put the fully loaded bag onto the scale at home, and I was delighted when I found it only weighed eighteen pounds. Now, however, it seemed it was very heavy. Worse yet, my turmoil was being watched, though I didn't even know it.

I looked up, and a tall, slim, and utterly handsome man who looked like he had just fallen out of a print ad had noticed my dilemma. He was sauntering my way as my cheeks flushed deep red.

He turned to me, asking in a dreamy Australian accent, "Do you need some help?"

Somewhat shocked that an exotic Ken doll had just spoken to me, I was embarrassed that I was having such a hard time with my own luggage.

I didn't quite know what to say, and awkwardly replied, "Oh, I think I've got it!"

But then, giving the situation a second thought, I blurted out, "I probably need a lot of help."

I added a quick look of despair, a smile, and a glance toward his too-handsome face. His chiseled jawline and sparkly eyes seemed too good to be true. Being a complete gentleman, he accepted my cue and quietly stepped around to the back of me without any fuss and lifted my backpack off my body, then handed it to me.

I marveled at how good it felt to accept this gesture, and I watched him as he walked away to the front of the line. I took a while to reorganize my luggage, but all the while I had one eye looking at where he had gone, and I was thinking, *darn, I wish I knew where he was seated.* I giggled inwardly; my first response after hearing his Aussie accent had been to turn into an instant crazed stalker!

One of my friends, Mike, had told me that the people down under would love my accent, but wow, I didn't realize until now how I felt about theirs. Endless possibilities of romance started to stir in my imagination.

I connected to Brisbane, and on the flight, I had an aisle to my right and an empty seat to my left, with plenty of space to stretch out and relax. I was glad I had pre-ordered vegetarian meals, delightful dishes filled with beans, pasta, and loads of tomatoes. At this point, I confess I was tempted to have a glass of wine with my dinner. Sometimes, I like to have a drink, but today I looked around and saw the others who were drinking, the thought of a glass lost its appeal. Everyone looked so lifeless as they put cocktails or wine up to their lips. Instead, I decided sleep was more valuable than dehydration from alcohol, so made the choice of two rarely used regular Tylenol for my body to relax. These knocked me out for a good long nap.

When I woke up, I still had enough time to watch four movies, including the new *Mary Poppins*. This was my third twelve-hour-plus flight in my life, and I'm not saying it is my favorite pastime, but now that I'd discovered high-quality knit compression socks really do work, it was almost enjoyable.

The long flight gave me plenty of time to daydream about finding a healing drum circle and fantasize about scuba diving the Great Barrier Reef. I planned to stay close to the divemaster; no trusting dive buddies who might have less experience than me. I couldn't have any mishaps at this point in my life, since I had a mother to come home to, and she was expecting 6:00 a.m. lattes.

From Brisbane, there was another connection to make, this time to Cairns. We landed there around 10:40 a.m. on Good Friday, April 19, 2019. Customs hardly even noticed my arrival, and I was waved straight through. The airport was small and easy to master, so I soon found the ground transportation section, hopped into a cab, and headed toward the hotel on Abbot Street; in fact, it was The Abbott, a boutique hotel that had looked lovely online. The main reason for selecting it was that I liked its location. It stood one block from the ocean and one block from the river.

As I rode in the cab toward City Central, I watched the Google map I had carefully studied come alive. I could feel the warmth surrounding my body, and my skin joyfully sucked in the damp air, precious gifts from the sea and the tropics. My heart was filled with joy. I felt good, giggling with delight to myself that I had taken the word of a crow, and now I was feeling very accomplished and deeply grateful.

The boutique hotel was located between the megastore Woolworth's and a high-end jewelry store. Because it was a public holiday, many of the Cairns shops were closed, including the Woolworth's, and this was a little disappointing. The hotel clerk had told me I could grab a nice meal there, and I was hungry.

Anyway, I checked into the clean, crisp boutique hotel that turned out to be every bit as nice as it had looked online. My research had also indicated it would be in a convenient location, accessible to shops, restaurants, and the boat docks for transportation to the reef and nearby islands. I had wanted to make sure I was very comfortable for at least the first two nights, ensuring I would get really good rest after traveling across the world. This proved to have been a great decision.

I bathed to wash off the stickiness and grime of travel, basking in the steam and the warm water. I dressed in gauzy full-legged pants and a tank top. Then headed out to wander the blocks toward the sea. Some restaurants and shops were open, and I read a chalkboard menu on the sidewalk in front of an open-patio restaurant showing breakfast specials; this gave me an idea of the cost of a meal. At first, it seemed a little high, but then with calculating the lower-valued Australian dollar, it wasn't bad at all, and it was definitely not as pricey as where I had come from, Southern California. I went into a clothing shop to just look around; retail fashion has always been a hobby for me. Then I decided I'd better start asking questions. The crow had sent me here because I was a healer, and now I was ready to meet other healers like me; I was also feeling that I personally needed healing and wanted to find my people.

Determined to find spiritual support, I asked a lady in a dress shop, "Do you know anyone that does drum circles around here?"

She smiled and gestured across the street. "They have drums over there."

I looked across the boulevard and saw a sign: Didgeridoos. I was already familiar with these, since their vibration sounds were used by healers in my yoga community. I'd had my first didgeridoo healing at the Bakti Festival in Joshua Tree, California, in 2014. The vibration had filled my body, penetrating my sore hip and upper thigh. I had pulled my hamstring a few weeks before the festival—stupidly, by slipping on a towel at a Bikram yoga demonstration at Macy's department store—and I really felt this sound healing had been very beneficial in my recovery.

My feelings were that the ancient wind instrument healing had caused a great improvement in my leg. I had lain on the ground in a vendor's booth filled with crystals while a man played the wind instrument over my body. The vibration filled my core, and I felt the warmth move though me. After he was done playing, he told me not to eat bad food. I have been wondering ever since then, what is bad food? Baby cow, pigs, french fries, or real real junk food like Jack in the Box?

It was clear to me, anyway, why someone would point out a didgeridoo shop. After all, I was in Australia, the birthplace of this amazing eucalyptus branch instrument, and as far as I knew, it was used for healing.

I left the dress shop and walked down toward the ocean, where I found the huge public pool called the Esplanade Lagoon. I had discovered this pool while doing internet research on the city and had instantly felt attracted to the idea of going there. It had a sand shore on one side and was about one hundred meters long with huge angelfish sculptures growing out of the deeper end. There was also an infinity edge on the side that faced the ocean, and it was actually more beautiful than I expected. I would swim laps in this pool for about five hours during my two-week visit to Cairns. Because there wasn't access to the ocean, it was the only way I could swim.

When I first arrived at the huge pool, there were little fluffy gray clouds in the sky, and the breezy fall weather was still very warm. I had anticipated this with knowledge from my research of the region.

I stood there and looked toward the sea; it was just as Zanna had told me. There was no beach, since this area was actually swampland where the tree groves had met the ocean. The sea in front of the town was met by muddy silt, exposed by the constant removal of the trees that would fill the coast with dense vegetation if not interfered with. This muddy area was left to the local wildlife to patrol.

I took in the vast openness of the sea and the soft clouds in the blue-gray sky. Then, after I had explored the park and pool area, I headed back down the block to the didgeridoo shop that had been pointed out to me. I entered the shop, admiring the Aboriginal art on the walls and the racks of the carved and painted ancient-style native wind instruments ranging from about three-and-a-half feet to about ten feet in length and painted with high-contrast tribal graphics.

A small bench stood across from where the salesman was, and I took off my day pack, placed it on the bench, and sat down. Here, I had a bird's-eye view of the handsome salesman. I also noticed that there were no drums in the shop. Feeling a bit like a creepy alien that had just dropped into the shop to take up residence, I sat and listened to the salesman as he pitched his wares to tourists being sucked in off the promenade by the interesting shapes and colors of the wind instruments.

The shopkeeper was a tall, thick, broad-shouldered man, and he had light hair shaved close to his head. He was wearing a sleeveless black button-down shirt, khaki pants, and flip-flops. Now he was demonstrating the didgeridoo to a young couple. The sounds swirled in the air with ups and downs as he spoke the word *crocodile* while vibrating his lips and releasing air into the instrument.

"Every one of these digeridoos has a unique sound. No two are alike. They are carved out by termites," he said while holding the five-foot-long instrument, resting one end on the floor and putting the other end up to his lips.

A warm vibrating sound came out of the eucalyptus tree branch. He flashed a smile as he reached for a smaller instrument and then gestured for a young man to try, who then demonstrated with his own full lips, vibrating them loosely while he let a small amount of air pass through them at the same time. His gray-green eyes lit up as he smirked a reaction to the customer's feeble attempt to play, making noises more like a cow passing gas than musical notes. They all laughed and giggled, and he patiently described and then demonstrated the breath and lip technique again.

I listened from my perch and watched as he spoke to interested shoppers. His voice was dreamy, his smile large as he gave each potential buyer a quick lesson on the exotic wind instrument, pointing at the racks of eucalyptus branches, explaining how they had been hollowed out by termites, carved, and then painted with tribal designs by an Aboriginal elder. It felt really good to be there, sitting on the small bench in the corner of the room. By now, the shopkeeper had noticed me watching him, and I caught him giving me quick glances as he demonstrated his well-practiced sales skills.

After a while, he started small talk with me. "Where are you from?"

I answered while checking his hand for a wedding ring. "California, have you ever been there?"

The conversation continued, and I really enjoyed his accent. He smiled and, in turn, seemed to very much enjoy my many stories about me being sent to do healings. He was very receptive to everything I said. He even had a spray bottle filled with essential oils and water that he had blended to use as a body and room spray, something I had also been doing the past few years.

As I left the shop, I thought, *there are no drums here, but still very interesting.*

I went by the shop later that day after my swim, and also Saturday after my swim. By Sunday evening, he had invited me to the beach. We drove up to Trinity

Beach, then walked a path out to the point, lighting our way with our cell phones. Here I was, on a path to a beach in the dark where crocodiles lived. I didn't let on that I was nervous as the dark path wound around the bush-covered hillside to the seaside cliff, although as I rounded each bend, I was thinking I might walk into a large crocodile. I tried to appear relaxed as I analyzed the situation.

Daniel—my lovely escort's name—had been born and raised here, and he was still alive and hadn't yet been mauled by crocodiles. I needed to just trust in him and enjoy the experience. We sat on the cliff with the bright moon in the sky, so bright I could see stringy clouds in its glow. The sea was pounding against the cliff below us, and there was a chilly wind. I had bought jeans earlier that day and was thankful for long pants and my pink three-quarter-length windbreaker, but still, I wasn't really equipped for cold weather. I had been expecting weather in the mid-eighties, but I had brought the windbreaker along anyway to keep me warm after diving. Thank goodness for that; we were out there on a bench for a long time, and I was enjoying his company, but finally I announced I was too cold. Even curling up next to him wasn't keeping me warm enough with that wind. Daniel drove me back to the hostel that I had opted for when I left the Abbot, just behind the City Central Mall. A great location, as this was where all the bus stops were and the train depot to Kurunda.

One day, I took the bus to Kurunda on a round trip. Sky rails and trains, the other options, were not important to me. Riding the public transit was much more the type of adventure I was seeking. I sat on the very back raised bench and enjoyed chatting with a fellow traveler, a female chemist from London; she was truly interested in my perfumes for protection and healing work. The half-hour trip up the curvy mountain road passed quickly, and we arrived at the village, which consisted of a collection of brightly colored touristy-looking shops. I went inside the market and found a latte. Then I walked around outside the shops and found a marked nature-walk trail that took me down to a wide river where the path was lined with very old-looking huge, thick-trunked eucalyptus trees. I was wondering if I was going to see a crocodile. Then

I came to a small dock, and a woman was standing on the end about to untie a boat that looked like something out of a Disneyland ride. It had a white canopy top and red railing around the sides. There were three couples on board.

I yelled out to her, "May I join?"

She smiled and waved me aboard, so I ran down the dock, not to hold up the starting of the river cruise. I quickly found a seat on an empty aluminum bench and saw there were swallows nesting on the boat in the canopy top that kept swooping and fluttering between us guests. I chuckled to myself; better than Disneyland.

First stop directly across from the dock was a wild cassowary, a truly rare sight; this flightless bird is not quite as large as an ostrich, but it's considered the most dangerous living bird in the world. I giggled when our guide described how this bird could rip your stomach out, while at the same time she fed this giant bird, Elvis, some fish food, mentioning that he probably was a little out of sorts because she hadn't brought him any fresh fruit. The boat was only a couple of feet from the shore, and this was already a real show worth the $20 AUD.

Next, on the left bank, we saw "freshies," freshwater crocodiles. Our guide explained to us these freshwater crocodiles were timid, nothing like their known-to-be-man-eating salty cousins. She assured us she swam in this river all summer long.

We went back to the dock, and I hiked back up the suspended bridges to the village. The village of shops were just closing up, and I found my way back to the bus stop and I rode back down to Cairns.

This was the only nearby tourist attraction I felt I needed to see. So now, it was time to venture out of Cairns. I was excited about this. The crow had made it clear I was to travel around the area, not just stay in one place.

So, I executed a trip to the very remote place known as the Cape Tribulation, making the three-hour drive in a four-wheel-drive public-transit bus, complete with a ferry crossing of a very wide river. My arrival at my new accommodations in the oldest rainforest in the world was perfectly timed to catch a horseback tour to the beach, quite an experience splashing through the warm waters on horseback.

I stayed in this area for two nights, the most grounded place I'd ever been on Earth, where the rainforest jungles that were filled with giant trees and vines met the flat, sandy beaches. These beaches had signs posted not to enter the water, with pictures of crocodiles. I made selfie videos, joking about how the beach was so crowded, so I couldn't take off my top. In actuality, I had caught the only two people sharing the miles of shore with me in the background of my recording. I drank in Mother Earth's grounding energy, thinking, *well, there's definitely an imbalance. This is truly the most completely grounded I've ever felt anywhere. This is an experience I would love to drag others to. A great place for healing workshops.*

I returned to Cairns and continued enjoying the markets with all their delicious foods and wares. Daniel and I enjoyed meals together, and one night I did a healing for him. It was very interesting because he appeared on the other side as a large frog. I also saw in my mind's eye the head of an Aboriginal man smiling down at me as I worked. I assumed that because he was smiling, it was a good sign.

The hostel I was staying at was filled with young people. I made friends with a girl from the US who was considering a trip to India for her two hundred–hour yoga-teacher training. After we chatted one day, she booked the trip to India, but before she left, I guided a yoga session on the hostel's deck by the pool, for her and another guest.

It was amazing because as we lay down for our final resting pose, flying above us were the huge bats that would take flight every evening from the trees near the library in the city center to the nearby hills, going off to hunt. I also did a healing for her before she left, and again as I worked, I saw the Aborigine—I can only assume spirit guide—smiling down at me. I enjoyed all my time in Australia. It's a very wild, expansive country with a lot more nature than I am accustomed to.

As the crow from Crow Nation had instructed me to practice my healing work while in Cairns, one day, I sat cross-legged on the small bed in my private hostel room, wearing my pale-gold headset, and I found shamanic drumming on YouTube. After seven years of walking on the other side, I now understood clearly that

I was going to other dimensions to do my healing work. I had first been introduced to drumming at the weekend workshop with Art Runningbear in 2013. This was the workshop where I'd made my own deerskin healing drum. After we'd completed our drums, we gathered in the living room for a drum healing circle. Art demonstrated how to watch the body language of your client and compose your drumming to match their energy.

That day, when it was my turn, I lay in the middle of the circle with my eyes closed. I saw a theme that would become a common thread for my journeys, a large fire pit with people gathered around it. In my imagination, I danced to the beat of the drum, changing the rhythm of my movement as the drumbeats quickened. I was jumping and twirling with an elaborate red costume on, its long strips moving violently to the fast-paced drumming as I spun and leaped. I don't remember Art calling this a journey, but I found when I practiced drumming for my dad, he had a story to tell me of where he had been while I drummed for him. This made me aware that people traveled in their minds while listening to the drums.

I listened to the sound of the drums, the cue for my mind to drop into the journey. In my mind's eye, I searched the nearby landscape and went back to the crystal cascade waterfalls Daniel had taken me to the day prior. There, I entered a cave on the side of the river, climbed down into the caverns, and dropped down into the lower world. I ran through the tunnel, then a meadow, then came to a volcano, dived in, and went down, down, and down, then came up to the apex of Cape Tribulation. When I came out of the top of the mountain, there was a ladder for me to go across to a huge ship in the ocean. I called out to the clusters of souls I could see hanging around. I watched the ship filling with the souls that wanted to go to an upper-world. Then I guided the whole ship up safely though the interworld and then up to the first level of heaven.

I giggled to myself because in the shamanic Death and Beyond workshop, that I'd attended the week before I left the US, I had been instructed to only take one soul at a time to their preferred destination, lower-world or upperworld. I thought, *geez what a rebel! Here I am, gathering and moving hundreds of souls and being bossy, taking them to the upperworld!* I went back the same way I had come, popping out back at the waterfall at the crystal cascade. Then I flew above the ground to the Esplanade, where I sat cross-legged on the grass.

With all my heart, I began whirling and twirling, cleaning with fairy dust all over to send love and harmony throughout the city. I wrapped up all the darkness and sent it out to the sea. I danced with my shaman spirit guides, burned the city down, and sent love throughout the ashes, watching as the city reappeared, glistening with the sparkly love. I filled my heart and everyone's nearby with love. I found a frog totem and merged with it, hopping around the city, smashing out all the evil. I flowed love and new growth to the whole city.

Then I rested and brought my energy back to myself from everywhere. I filled myself with the power of the frog and looked at the city in its entirety. I brought Mother Earth up and Father Sky down, so they would be brought back together in harmony here at the river mouth. I brought the forest and the river energy back to the sea and merged them as one. Then, content with my work, my duties completed, I swirled ribbons of rainbows, signing my work with the words *Rainbow Dancer*.

Let me just stress again here that this description is not intended to be used as a guide to attempt this type of work on your own. I have years of experience and well-practiced skills of protection.

What I'm trying to emphasize is special things happen when you are true to your guides, true to your higher self. It may not be for everyone to give up your home and travel the earth alone to bring your healing light to faraway places, but there are so many worlds within our earth, and while you are having this experience, I'm encouraging you to travel. I marvel at the special things that happened when I was true to my guides and my higher self.

On my last day in Cairns, I was sitting at the Black Bird coffee shop on Ocean Walk, my chest heaving, my eyes welling up. My emotions had all surfaced, but I was filled with the contentment of my experience.

I had trusted my guides and received so much joy in doing so. I had gotten on a plane and flown to the other side of the world, and all this because I listened to a crow. I listened to my higher self and guides. I felt it gave me an advantage over the rest of the world. I took the suggestions of the crow and experienced a trip of a lifetime with perfect timing. All this because I followed guidance from the metaphysical world.

I did have the thoughts of, if all else fails, at least I will get to dive the Great Barrier Reef, but this was an amazing trip; the connection with the frog was very empowering. Just before I left Cairns, I discovered a plaque in the streets that told the story of how developers had found evidence in the area Aboriginal healers working with frog medicine. Fascinating.

CHAPTER 6

End of May

It was a challenge to get to San Jose after two weeks of bar life, and now I sat with my sister in a conference room with about thirty other inquisitive persons, in an institution located in San Mateo.

Red Wing's author's lecture unfolded perfectly, like a blooming rose. She told the stories of humans leaving this lifetime and explained clearly what a sacred process it is. We enjoyed the soul-touching tales laced with humor and love, as she brought animation to the writings contained in her book, *Last Acts of Kindness*. My sibling got caught up with the author, a childhood friend, and we took pictures with the signed copies of the book and author.

The next step in my yogic sister's plan was to head to the Santa Cruz Mountains. We had eaten amazing Himalayan food late in the afternoon, but we had only shared one dish. Now I was getting hungry, and my head had started to ache. I had chosen not to have coffee that day, my reasoning being that this would help me adapt to a daylight time schedule for the weekend. For the past two weeks, I had been drinking up to two cups of coffee before my night shift, with hope that I would be alert enough to engage with others at the nightclub.

We arrived at the motel too late for dinner. I was hungry, thirsty too, and my head hurt. I walked over from the room to the motel bar, determined there was no food available, and ordered myself a beer. Fermented hops and barley sounded better than only water for dinner. Sure enough, the beer filled me up, and I was comfortable in the familiar environment of the bar.

One customer and a bartender and I all sat together in the well-stocked motel bar; the other customer had just returned from his home in Mexico, where he had enjoyed an extended vacation, and they were catching up. The bartender was petite in stature, brunette, with sexual energy bubbling out of her. She was a transplant from Rhode Island and had an opinion about everything. I found it amusing that each time I would say something, she would come back with some strong story, bringing the focus right back to herself.

I said, "I really like to scuba dive!"

She replied, "Oh, I love the ocean! I go down and look at it almost every day, but I don't go in, because I'm scared of sharks." She backed this up with a story coming from somewhere in Florida, about a man-eating bull shark that turned up in a depth of only four feet of water.

This brought my mind to June of 2007, when I had jumped into the flat waters of the blue Caribbean, preparing for the La Jolla one-mile rough-water swim. The inviting water motivated me to dive right off the grounded sloop that I was crewing on and swim for forty-five minutes. The warm swim was amazing, but we ended up stuck on that sandbar for a few hours until the tide changed. After that, I spent most of our sailing time keeping a close eye on the electronic depth monitor. I was amused by the captain's story that this boat had been grounded on the sandbars in the shallow waters near Marsh Harbor so many times that the good-humored owner had suggested renaming the sloop from *Clueless* to *Groundhog*.

Sharks—lemon sharks to be exact—were number two on shark week list, shown in the sea-grass-filled seascape that I had enjoyed for ten days of swim training off the *Clueless* deck. I thought, *ugh, now shark week has ruined that swim spot for me. Where in the world can I ocean swim?* Since I'd been a teenager in the seventies, I would reluctantly join my mother and her friends to swim to the half-mile buoy loop just outside of La Jolla Cove, San Diego. I was convinced great whites were lurking below in those deep canyons beneath us. I had felt so much safer in the shallow, bright aqua waters, but the shark week list had ruined that.

I told the bartender and the customer, "I like scuba diving with sharks. I always feel much safer under the water than splashing around on the surface."

She added she knew a gal who got carbon dioxide poisoning while scuba diving in Mexico and almost died. I thought while she told the story, *so, no one else got sick from supposed bad air?* My mind wandered to deaths from diving that I personally knew about.

Tired of the morbid topic now filling my head, I came back to the present time and studied my surroundings; the bar was filled with shiny bottles placed against a mirror background. The place felt safe and familiar, my mind echoing years of sitting at the club bar when there were either no customers or too many. I felt a little high from the quickly consumed locally brewed ale; by now, I could still feel my headache but honestly didn't care about the dull ache anymore. The bartender offered me another beer, but as comfortable as it all felt, I made a decision to go back to the room.

My sister had already climbed into the king-sized, white-sheeted bed, and she had added the extra blanket from the closet over the already fluffy down comforter.

It was late May, and I was thankful for the heavy bedding. I thought as I climbed under the covers, *California coast is beautiful, but it sure is damp and cold.* I put my head onto the pillow and wondered how I was going to sleep after weeks of working into the night.

The room lightened as the sun rose, and I hadn't slept

much at all. I felt dehydrated, and the dull headache had taken over my entire skull. I was relieved when my sibling rose early and wanted to find breakfast. I used my Yelp app on my cell phone and found a place that was open at 7:00 a.m. When we got there, they were not actually serving breakfast, but they had this amazing deli case stuffed with burritos, gluten-free quiche and—my choice—a spinach-and-cheese croissant.

My sister chose the same. As I ate my stuffed croissant, I reminisced about the same delicious choice at market in Cairns the month before. That day, I had followed up with a petite lemon meringue pie for dessert. Today, I was skipping the pie or cake that I had been finding myself eating so frequently, but I ordered a decaf latte with almond milk, hoping it would ease my headache. After breakfast, my sister drove me back to our motel so I could go back to bed. With a pastry-filled belly and my sister off to visit her college best friend, I slept well until just before our noon checkout time.

We decided there was enough time to head to the Mount Madonna Center and visit the Hindu temples. As we arrived, I was bitching about a couple of family members. My sister marched across Hanuman's temple on her way to Ganesh's temple in her shoes, looking back at me and telling I wasn't allowed to talk about my annoying family. She had lived at the Mount Madonna, and she was very aware of the customs. I judged her. I repeatedly thought as I was trying to clear my mind for prayer. This girl was so busy scolding me that she walked through sacred space with her shoes on.

I settled in and sat staring at the carved wooden sign above Hanuman. I took a few breaths, feeling this was a timely visit and grateful that my sister had brought me to the spiritual center. I had spent thirty days in Rishikesh, India, in what I like to call Hindi kindergarten, also known as two hundred–hour yoga-teacher training. In India, the temples had been extremely colorful and filled with strange deities. There was a woman with many arms, a man with a monkey head, and there had been dark-skinned, dark-eyed men asking for donations, offering a gift of plastic prayer beads in trade. I wasn't comfortable in the temples when I was there, and I'm sure I looked very much like an awkward outsider with my platinum-blonde hair and fair skin.

But now I sat in California in front of the monkey god after four years of yogic practice, teaching, and study. I was truly grateful that I could pray to Hanuman for strength to complete a body of written work, with no attachment to the outcome. I chanted the Asatoma mantra, as I stared at the carved words. This is the only prayer my masters in India had succeeded in me memorizing, but of course with terrible pronunciations. I chanted the purifying prayer quietly to myself with my intention.

My sister soon collected me, and we headed down the path, stopping at the coffee shop, where I got a large mint tea, and then we walked down the path to the Ayurvedic shop, where I purchased some pure organic oils for my perfume-making. My following of perfume clients were expecting something fantastic for my summer edition, and my supplies were low. The high-quality oils proved to be just what I needed. I stocked up on the precious oils, and now it was time to head to our retreat.

We drove up the winding road to Scotts Valley. My sister had planned and booked us a weekend retreat at

1440 Multiversity, the most expensive spiritual-growth school in California. I was assuming that would mean beautiful grounds and resort-like accommodations, and I was not disappointed. There was valet luggage service, complete with bright-eyed staff, and gorgeous redwood buildings with blue-gray slate roofs and copper details. The structures elegantly blended into the surrounding redwood forest. This institution had been built with Silicon Valley money, so abundant that the individuals from there had developed their own unique trend of understated elegance. My mind collected all the details, huge granite rocks forming fire pits, waterfalls, and fountains. The granite rocks had been cut with artisan skill. My mind calculated there had to have been visionaries, designers, and true craftsmen; I knew it took a tremendous amount of work to build anything, but this was a work of art. This elite construction, combined with the fact it was a school of spiritual healing and growth, created a magic that I had never seen before in the world.

My sister navigated the path to our room. I climbed the ladder to the top bunk of the train-car-style accommodations and dropped my duffel bag. I dug into my luggage. There I found a yoga bra and a bathing suit thong bottom. I wanted to get into the therapeutic hot pool, but I questioned the appropriateness of my attire. I was still dealing with what I had packed two weeks ago. I made the decision that I would survey the situation at the pool area, then decide whether or not I might take off my midi, gray-hooded sweatshirt dress. It was late in the afternoon and the warmest it had been all day. I put a towel on a lounge chair as I looked around the pool area. Across the way were a couple of middle-aged women engrossed in conversation. In the 101-degree pool, one couple stood leaning against the side wall, but what really caught my attention—because he looked a little out of place—was the one middle-aged man fully dressed in the far corner of the patio area, near the outdoor shower. He was on his cell phone.

I took off my dress and quickly sat down on the lounge chair. I took a few deep breaths trying to relax, glad I had my prescription sunglasses on but still feeling I was missing a hat to protect my face from the late-afternoon sun. I had that sticky, dusty feeling from being out and about all day and wanted to rinse off in the outdoor shower, but there was the fully dressed man, lurking around only five feet from the shower.

My mind wandered to an outdoor beach shower I had taken in Miami a few years ago when I was with a gaggle of gals for a bachelorette party. Oblivious to my surroundings, I had rinsed off the salt and sand of a half-hour ocean swim and returned to my gang. The girls giggled and squeaked with delight, saying they were going to marry me off to the old man who had been ogling me during my shower. They added their perceived advantage of the union between me and the voyeur, a beach condo in Miami so they could come visit. How had I not noticed there was some creepy old man watching me? I was so embarrassed!

But the option of living in Miami sounded interesting, so I said, "If you guys are going to marry me off, could you please find me a handsome man without the creepy shower-stalking habits?"

Now here at 1440 Multiversity, I had to decide whether to break the discipline of a shower before entering a pool and just sneak straight into the hot pool, or I could wrap myself in my towel, walk over to the shower and act like it was perfectly appropriate for me to rinse off in a thong and a yoga bra with a fully clothed man on his cellphone five feet away. I went for the shower, but premeditated a quick rinse. As I walked over, wrapped safely in my towel, I observed my fully clothed man soon to be my audience. He had light-brown curly hair and weeks of unshaven scruff. His upper body appeared thick, and he was a little taller than average. He was wearing a button-down shirt and slacks. An interesting combination: dress clothes and a scruffy face. I decided he must have just arrived from a workplace that he owned. I imagined he was on the phone with an employee, finishing up last-minute Friday afternoon business, before he got into his weekend of self-discovery.

A quick rinse and then I sank into the warm pool, and this got me out of my head and present with my experience. I leaned over the infinity edge of the pool, taking in the view of the majestic redwoods.

I left the total bliss and walked to the other side of the campus. There I joined the Qigong class that my yogic sister had insisted would be good for me. My body was tired, and the movements hurt my arms, plus it was a challenge to listen to the teachers instructions and stay with the class. I got hot, and I was relieved when it was over, still not convinced it had been good for me.

I headed to the dining hall, excited to experience dinner, but the best part of the meal was meeting Meredith. She had also been in the Qigong class and had also gotten too hot in it, so already we had something in common. Plus, she was also at 1440 for the weekend. We immediately engaged in conversation, and she was open and light. She was dealing with fear—to be precise, the fear of loss of control of her normally tightly reined-in emotions. I liked her honesty and found her refreshing to be around. We talked and ate.

My sister had chosen to eat on the silent side of the dining hall. Well, I had no desire to eat in silence and enjoyed making a new friend. The silent diner finished her meal then joined me back at my table, and we decided to collect sweaters back at our room. However, poor time management resulted in us showing up five minutes late to the first class.

Mortified, I slowly entered the room and took the last seat available just to the right of the facilitator of the class. Wendy was telling a concise and interesting backstory, and the energy in the room was warm and comforting. She then requested for each of us to give our name and our one word of intention for the workshop. I was surprised when the woman to my right of me chose the word *kundalini*. My imagination flashed with an image of a snake uncoiling out of her stomach and striking into the air.

I repeated her word back to her and added, "That's some one word."

And then I said, "Detachment."

Wendy guided us into the earth with an elevator, a practice I'm familiar with and use quite a bit. I was introduced to it by Jeffrey Allen in 2014. But today my elevator stopped in the interworld. I had not made it to the beautiful and nurturing lower world, and Mother Earth looked like the creepy witch. She wasn't handing me a nurturing tea; she was trying to give me poison. I was familiar with the beautiful Mother Earth and knew this wasn't her.

I'd already had an amazing experience during a healing I had done for a friend last year, and so the vision Wendy was describing to the class had previously shown itself to me. But today I was seeing scary things. I was calm though. I had no fear of the low-vibration entities trying to block the light Wendy was offering. Perhaps the low vibrations of the universe were feeling threatened as I was growing stronger. These creepy visions had started in San Luis Obispo at the Foundation of Shamanic Studies' Death and Beyond workshop in April, just before I had traveled to Australia. I was trying to find my deceased grandmother Sylvia on the other side, and my teacher explained that stuck in the interworld, things might not look nice. It was not a place you wanted to hang out. It may be the closest thing to hell, as it is described by Christianity.

That day it had been very upsetting to me that there was a massacre of my favorite group of little healers, that I call "the Rainbow Healers of Light," a group of light-hearted, joyful, pixielike, but also extremely talented healing masters. This slaughter had been shown to me in my drug-free journey during that workshop. This had made me feel that I needed some sort of healing in my personal inner world. I'd been doing some research to find a healer and was looking at a shamanic practitioner in La Mesa near my parents' home.

But meanwhile, my life had been pretty well scheduled. San Luis Obispo Beyond Death workshop, two weeks in northeast Australia, two weeks in San Diego, including a Peruvian prayer ceremony. Now, a weekend in the California redwoods at a spiritual workshop.

This class had been advertised as an intuition-building workshop, and Wendy reasonably began the class with a grounding meditation, bringing the group into the Mother Earth. She then introduced us to our ancestors in the lower world.

As quickly as the scary visions had appeared, they melted away, and my familiar group of ancient shamanic practitioners showed themselves. Glad to see each other, we all were sitting around the fire, getting caught up. I was deep and comfortably seated in the womb of Mother Earth when suddenly the woman seated next to me in the room let out a loud yelp! Completely startled, I gasped.

Then with eyes wide open, I turned to Wendy and said, "That scared the shit out of me!"

And then I closed my eyes and dropped back into a trance and my journey. Wendy kindly moved over behind me and put her hands on my shoulders, offering my body a grounding healing. I accepted it and was grateful. Her energy felt sweet and pure. We finished up our journeys as the first session ended.

As I was leaving the room, I noticed a cute guy in an Australian graphic T-shirt. What is it about me and Aussies? I headed to the patio fire pit nearby. Meredith was there and had already settled into the enjoyment of a mason jar of Chardonnay. I arrived at the fire pit bursting with the story.

"Oh my God," I cried. "That was crazy. I was deep in my journey and just getting comfortable around a fire with my normal crew of ancestral healers when the lady next to me let out a yelp. It scared the shit out of me. I let out quick scream, just like I would when a swamp monster jumped out of the TV at me."

We both giggled.

"Sooo embarrassing!" I went on. "The teacher felt she needed to give me a healing, and I was glad she did. I can still feel the adrenaline in my bloodstream.

Nothing like this ever happened to me before!"

It was all very true, after seven years of group meditations. They were definitely something I always found safety in, but now, that belief was shattered.

I immersed myself into my group of peers surrounding the firepit.

"So, what's going on out here?" I inquired.

I looked across the fire, where three young women were sitting with notebooks in their hands and a jar of rose wine on their redwood lounge chair.

Meredith said, "These are the Lululemon gals; they are in yoga-teacher training."

"Nice!" I said, enthused. "Is this your three hundred–hour?"

The second yoga student said, "No. We are just doing our two hundred–hour training."

"What are you studying right now?" I asked.

Number three yoga student piped up, "We are preparing to teach a class with a theme."

"What are the examples of themes?" I asked.

The bright-eyed, slim-faced, and soft-brown-haired, yoga-attired executive went ahead and listed the examples.

My favorite among the list was gratitude.

The gals introduced themselves.

We giggled a lot. Meredith explained she was a human resources director for a megacorporation. We all bathed in each other's warm, energetic auras. The girls attending the two hundred–hour yoga training had close to thirty years' combined experience in yoga apparel. I felt comfortable. It was a nice change from all the tension of my sister's expectations of me. These ladies were bright and confident. I relaxed and melted right into the conversations with joy.

The next day, I woke up early but didn't meet Meredith as planned at 7:00 a.m. for meditation. It was 6:55 a.m. by the time I checked my iPhone. I didn't want to walk in on a meditation class ten minutes after it started, but Meredith and I caught up around 8:15 a.m. at the Kitchen Table, the dining room that served all the food that was included with our housing. The food was good, and I was glad there were lentils and sweet potatoes for breakfast. It's not that I don't eat eggs; it was just that lentils and sweet potatoes take more time to prepare. Putting in no work to cook the food and yet getting the healthy food my body deserved made me smile. Meredith and I huddled on the far side of the fireplace, and I was enjoying her passion as she was catching me up on the important shifts in her life.

My sibling came by our table and stared at us for a while. She was still eating her meals on the far side of the dining room, shrouded in stony silence. This was where the two hundred–hour yogis were also taking their breakfast. So, after she ate, she would come by find me, and this time she stood at the end of the table, staring at us. I was sure this had some meaning to her. But I was enjoying my new best friend and sister scolding, and her neediness was wearing on me.

On arrival to 1440, I was expected to follow her blindly as she toured the campus, when I really just wanted to walk directly to the room on the route that I had already mapped out in my mind. When I questioned her route, she seemed annoyed that she had to explain to me again that we were walking by the dining hall. At that point, I really questioned my judgment about choosing to participate in this adventure. But I had taken a deep breath and realized she was just trying to be helpful and show me where I would find nutrition. My family all have big, kind hearts but so often seem to be working from a point of basic survival. This was something I didn't ever think about; from a young age, I had found anything I desired seemed to magically appear. It is hard for me to flow with my own family's vibration.

In the second day of the class, the Aussie and I were discussing the guided healing we had just experienced, creating a room in our second chakra to allow our toddler selves to dance, sing, scream, throw a tantrum, or just be excessively joyful. Basically, anything we may have been reprimanded for, or worse yet, ignored for as children. I had just asked him to share his experience of this deep work, and he was telling me what he had gone through, when my sister walked up next to us and stared at me again, not wanting it to look as awkward as it felt.

I asked, "How did your experience with the toddler in your second chakra go?"

She looked at me with a confused quick glance into my eyes and said, "I don't know what you are talking about."

It was a clear and well-explained exercise, so her response confused me. But I remembered earlier, she had told me the teacher had said it was okay for her to rest in the corner. She had explained to Wendy at the start of class that she had not slept well that night.

I covered for her by saying, "She was sleeping."

We broke to return to our seats, but before I could get away from my irritated sibling, she said, "That was very dismissive."

I was thinking I was trying to be kind and cover for her awkward comment! She was staring at me, expecting an apology, and I was doing everything I could to stay calm and not to just blurt out my defense. I made hand gestures to show that I was grounding myself. I took a deep breath; I'd just been accused of malice, and it was not that I didn't want to know why she felt this way, but it was more that class was starting. I quietly went to my nearby seat.

I tried everything to stay in my own space, but now my sister was scolding the Kundalini lady seated next to her for physically reaching out to offer her condolences. My sister was very upset. I had reached out with my hand to the yelper's knee after she had yelped.

Surely, it's natural to reach for someone who is in peril. Anyway, the class began, and right on cue, Wendy began teaching a technique for holding your own space while somebody else is in an emotional wreck.

I turned to Josie on my right, since there was no way I wanted to work with the yelper on my left. I needed a break, and I was sure Josie was the perfect antidote. She had joyful, light energy about her, her cool, clear-rimmed glasses projecting her hipness and framing her sparkling eyes, adding a perfect balance to her pink hair with natural roots. Josie had brought a journal to take notes, and I was envious of that, yet refreshed by just looking at her and next she added a huge warm embrace. I could feel the power of her love, and she even mentioned how she loved my sister.

We began the exercise, a roleplay. The assignment carefully explained by Wendy was as follows.

"You are riding the train next to each other, and one of you is upset over something, so the other one is to hold space using the grounding technique.

"The grounding person can observe the other's energy by using their lower chakras. But then you are to bring back all feelers and ground yourselves."

I volunteered to be the upset person first. Easily enough, I moved quickly into character, remembering the frustration I had just felt. I calmed quickly. Love radiated from Josie.

We switched roles, and now Josie's character entered the train and was silent. I reached with my lower chakras toward her, feeling grief. I collected my feelers and offered a permission rose, envisioning a rose between us. This offered her the right to her emotions and me the right to my space, but in this case, we had been instructed to ground ourselves, so I softened and slowed my breath and felt my body connect to the earth.

After a few moments. Josie released her upset character. She told me her intention had been frustration. I told her what I felt, and she agreed that my observation was possible, as she has had some recent grief in her life. Staying grounded and present when others were upset had been a huge challenge for me, and still is. I've noticed some improvement in the recent years but can still get knocked around by others' emotions. This was an excellent exercise to bring the skill into consciousness, and Josie was the perfect partner for me. We hugged, and I felt the love; we had enjoyed our time together.

It was time for lunch. On our way, my sister invited me to join her in a silent meal.

I responded with a quick "Fuck, no!"

This work was deep, and I needed to get out of my head and see the world through other people's eyes. I was proud of my yogic sister going for the silent meals, but I was enjoying getting to know the other souls drawn to 1440 for the weekend. I was finding it fascinating. I have spent tons of meals by myself in silence, and this was interaction time for me.

At lunch, I met up with Meredith. We were winding down when Aussie guy came over, sat on the hearth of the fireplace near me, and struck up a conversation. I moved over to the hearth next to him.

He asked me about my recent trip to Cairns. "How much time would it take to do healing in Australia?"

I was confused by his question and fumbled for a response. "I was sent there to do some personal healing on myself, and I did some healing on the area while I was there. I'm a healer."

Aussie said, "Let's see how good of a healer you are."

I responded, "I'm a good healer."

The Aussie began pouring out his fears about having children. I suggested a healing to connect his mind and heart, since to me, his heart and mind disconnected. He told me he would be here another twelve days, and I asked him how long he had been off work.

Aussie guy said, "I haven't worked in a year and a half."

This guy had passion and lots of it, and I inhaled it in as I sat next to him. I had noticed earlier he was wearing a wedding ring, so I was keeping the conversation as professional as possible.

Sister passed by the fireplace, looking at me intensely, making me uncomfortable. I caught Meredith glancing over to the Aussie and me too. I didn't mind when I felt her sweet curiosity of wonder. I am intuitive, and I always have been. It was not that I read people's minds; more like they put all their thoughts out in the ether.

This had made people uncomfortable in the past, me knowing their thoughts that they had not verbally expressed. But it helped in sales, and it had been an asset to my life. This weekend, my sister was loud with her neediness, and I was trying to figure out how to be patient with her and not let her emotions affect my joy, but it was a challenge. The class skills we were practicing were timely.

I asked the Aussie, "What are you seeking?"

I felt like he avoided the question because he evidently didn't feel comfortable sharing with me what was really going on. Instead, he talked about wanting to go to the hot pool, but it was close to one thirty, and class was starting at 2:00 p.m.

The thought flitted through my mind: was it that he just wanted to see me in a swimsuit again? I had finally realized the guy on his cell phone at the pool and my new classmate friend were the same guy.

He had already gotten a shower show, so what more did the guy want from me?

I dismissed myself to prepare to return to afternoon class and was saddened as I walked away, having lost the warm feeling of my new friend's engaging energy.

We returned to class, and Wendy explained the exercise for the healing of the fourth chakra, the heart chakra.

I did the work as presented, and I was thinking about Aussie guy and how this class had to be good for him too. The teacher was doing an amazing job and had already taught us to bring the Divine down though the backs of our bodies. Then she explained how, with discernment, one could open the rear door of each chakra to the Divine. Powerful!

Next, we moved to the fifth chakra, located in the throat area, and I went through the visualizations, adding a little prayer that I would be able to clearly express myself in the written word. The sixth chakra is in the center of our heads, where intuition comes from, and this was to be our next stop.

When you listened to your intuition, according to Wendy, that showed you were in balance. She taught us about the back side of the chakra, where we could connect to higher wisdom. I enjoyed that new awareness, and felt I was definitely going to put it to the test. Next, we headed to the crown chakra; she instructed us on how to open this area at the top of our heads like a funnel, and to let the Divine pour in. I like doing this with some discernment, maybe ask for a little filter of protection just to make sure you don't funnel anything unwanted. It felt good, since I hadn't let the Divine pour into me like this for a while. I felt familiar jolts as my body jumped within. Then I giggled to myself. Was this what made the Kundalini lady so noisy?

Anyway, everyone had unanimously agreed to add a session tonight at 7:30 p.m. for a guided integration meditation. When class broke, Josie and I found Meredith by the fire pit near the class hall. She had been keeping very busy. There was always plenty to do at 1440 without being enrolled in a course, such as Qigong, yoga, Pilates, guided meditations, and spa treatments. We tried to go to steam together, and Meredith was already checked in, so she went ahead into the spa. Josie and I were declined access, however, because the steam room was full. So, we walked down the trail and found the amphitheater. We had been talking the night before about Josie's writing group; I was so envious of this, as a group of friends to write with sounded delightful.

I walked onto the amphitheater stage to meet my challenge, which was impromptu poetry. I took a deep breath and could smell the damp, earthy forest. I listened, hearing the stream moving through the rocks just below the stage.

I began, "rippling water, damp air, towering trees, leaves catching waves of sunlight dancing above my head."

I sank into the space, letting it hold and support me, and I continued. "I stand in this beauty, feeling it swim through the cells of my body. How can war exist on a planet that feels like this?"

Josie applauded.

I said, "Now it's your turn."

She had a poem already composed on her phone. I listened intently to her melodic voice, marveling at the way she had strung the words together with her mind. But I missed the meaning, too busy enjoying listening to the beautiful sounds coming from her mouth.

We played a little longer, exploring down by the river edge and some nearby trails. Then we headed back toward our rooms, but just behind the building we were staying in, we ran into some other students from our class. After a quick visit, I decided to try heading back to the healing spa for a few moments in the eucalyptus steam room before going to dinner.

The extra evening session sounded easy enough, but it wasn't. The floor was cold and hard, and I wasn't dressed warmly enough. The meditation seemed familiar to me though, as if I had already done it before. My mind drifted back to India and a chilly 7:00 a.m. guided meditation. I was counting the minutes until it was over and wished I had just sat in a chair up off the cold floor. Finally, we were done.

I grabbed my thick woolen cardigan from the rack outside the classroom where my sister had hung it. I was very thankful for it and for the gesture that she had fetched for me after dinner. I went off to meet up with my buddies at the fire ring. The three yogis and Meredith were relaxed, enjoying wine and having a great time.

I said as I joined them, "Well, I didn't get to drink any wine in *my* two hundred–hour yoga training!"

Yogi number one said, "We've been told to relax. Apparently, we are taking this far too seriously."

Then she explained how yogi number two had gotten so upset over missing seven questions on the test earlier that day.

I asked, "How many questions were on the test?"

The yogi replied, "One hundred and twenty-seven."

Josie had joined us now. She and I both chimed in with lighthearted laughter. "That's good."

Then I added, "You guys are such type-A executives!" We all laughed.

It got late. We all headed to bed, but I didn't fall asleep. I was lit up, and that darn Aussie had been flirting with me every chance he got. He had even invited me to meet him at the hot pool after class, but I was seeing the bigger picture; he was in great need of a serious healing, and I had ethics.

Dream Aussie was reaching out, and I was here to serve. I decided as I moved into my dream world that tomorrow, I was going to enjoy his company but with complete ethics, and I wouldn't engage with him sexually. But I was going to find out what was going on with him and move the appropriate energy.

Frist thing—which wasn't early for me that day, as it was after 8:00 a.m.—I walked into the dining room and went straight over to the Aussie. "Good morning, handsome," I said.

Aussie guy said, "What?"

I confidently repeated myself. "Good morning, handsome."

He looked at me and smiled. "You didn't come to the hot tub last night?"

I said, "I was at the fire pit with my friends."

He asked, "What fire pit?"

"The one near our classroom."

I liked that he was asking me questions and was wondering where I had spent my time. My mind went back to the night before, and to hours of lying awake in my single bed. Ethics! How did I end up with this job? Healer. Ugh …

We were chatting about the workshop.

Aussie guy said, "I liked my last workshop better than this one; it was human intimacy."

He went into details of how the instructors were a divorced couple, and they were role playing. They demonstrated what adult consent looked like, and he told me it was like watching live porn. They were touching and caressing, complete with sounds. Then the class got to participate, and his partner was a drop-dead gorgeous woman!

He exclaimed, "I'm thinking, all my Christmases came at once!"

I smiled and thought to myself, *Aussies are so darn cute.*

He went on, "She tells me, do whatever you want. I'll let you know if you go too far."

Now I realized why his last workshop was better than the one we were in together. He had me giggling, telling me about the instructor's sex life. He called her an animal, and not with a derogatory tone. Her ex-husband lived in the basement of the house, and she rotated five lovers for her voracious sexual appetite.

I laughed as I confessed, "It always seems to me that the men I had relationships with who had the largest sexual appetites were crazy. I've often thought, why do I have to have insane men as partners?"

Aussie said, "I'm pretty sure that's me; crazy sexual guy."

Now he is letting me know he is my type! I was finding all of this so entertaining.

He mentioned open marriages, and I didn't question him, though I wondered what his wife's position was on this. I also noticed his wedding ring had been moved from this left hand to his right hand over the weekend. Or had it? Maybe I just didn't know my left from my right? Anyway, it didn't matter; he had made it clear he needed a healing. Ethics!

My sister stopped by and mentioned everyone else had headed to class. We smiled and waited till she left to continue our chat. He noticed I'd glanced at the clock.

He remarked, "We could spend hours talking, but I guess we should head to class."

My mind went to the thought of us talking all day, and it sounded great, but there were only a few precious hours left of the workshop. We headed to class, ten minutes late.

We joined the group, taking the two remaining chairs; being seated next to each other felt good. I felt great, my energy clear and strong. Wendy explained the assignment.

Person A was to hold space for person B, then ground into the earth with light to the center of the earth, and then lean into the divine light they were imagining flowing down their backside.

Person B was to also ground, open their crown chakra, and imagine divine light flowing down their back. They would open the back side of their throat chakra and their heart chakra to hear, see, and feel spirit messages or messages of higher knowing. Then they would look at their partner's light in the spirit world. I was person A first, so I did my job as instructed.

We switched, and this was the apex of the class; I was very anxious now.

What if I saw nothing? I followed the instructions, finding myself delighted with the Rainbow Healers of Light dancing in my head, all dressed up in white tulle, with veils. They were evidently excited, preparing for a celebration, and I giggled to myself. I found the Rainbow Healers of Light often reflected my actions. For example, if I was sitting in a dentist's chair, they would be dressed up as dentist, dental hygienist, and patients, with props included.

Two months ago, while I was in a journey at the Death, Dying, and Beyond workshop, there had been a bloody massacre of the whole group, and I hadn't seen them alive since. Every time I would go look for them, they were all still dead. It brought so much joy to my heart to see them alive now, and I didn't explain to them the love they were feeling really wasn't a cause for that much celebration. But they were right; I liked this guy.

He moved his toes on top of my feet, and I felt the energy pour into me. I thought, *rule breaker, that's not in the instructions.* It felt very good, though, and I didn't stop him. I felt my root and second chakra ignite, and I was joyful and amused, and those Rainbow Healers were all so right; there should be a wedding. I smiled to myself, delighted the Rainbow Healers of Light had come back to life.

We finished up the exercises, and Aussie, Wendy, and I walked out of the classroom together for a group picture. I chatted the news to Wendy that I had had a wonderful experience. The Aussie insisted it must be all because of him! I was laughing and saying it was because of her, due to her amazing program.

I did give him verbal praise for doing a great job of executing the skills she had introduced. After all, I was having a great time with him. I was standing with the Aussie when my sister cozied up to his other side.

Someone from the group shouted, "Look at the sisters. He has both sisters now, one on each side!" I was a little embarrassed, and then it got worse. The skinny—maybe twenty-two-year-old boy valet had arrived to take the group photo.

My sister leaned over to me behind Aussie's back and whispered loudly, "He is the hottest one!"

I glanced up and down the tanned young boy and thought, *why would she think that, never mind say it?* Suddenly now, she was acting like a perverse old lady when the Aussie could hear.

I didn't say anything in response, just pretended like it didn't happen.

Now, someone decided to move the whole group down the stairs we had been standing on, to a location just below next to a manicured garden, for more photos. My sister didn't join the group, announcing she was done with pictures. Slightly relieved, I wondered why, but didn't ask.

We went back into the classroom, and Wendy instructed the closing of the workshop. The class members broke into small chatting groups, while others scurried out the door. I decided it might be a good time to do some energy work on the Aussie. I set up a mat and pillows. He lay down, and I added a blanket over his clothed body. I wanted him relaxed and feeling safe. I prepared the already-amazing-feeling space. Then I gave a gratitude prayer and grounded myself.

I started with his head, gently placing my hands over each ear. I glanced at the clock and saw it was just a little after 11:15 a.m. I like to know what time it is when I start working. I sometimes lose track of the time in the altered state that I go into when doing a healing. Following my intuition, I moved to his shoulders. I wiggled around a little to get comfortable. It was difficult to give a healing on the ground, but he needed it. After about fifteen minutes, I moved straight to his feet. My intuition suggested to avoid his torso. I had informed him before we started that if at any time he was uncomfortable, to let me know so I could adjust what I was doing.

There were a few people in the room, and I could hear their topics of conversation; they were healing practitioners comparing notes about their practices.

They noticed the healing being performed and quieted down their conversation. I was at his feet, working a few different hand positions. I was looking at his torso and saw the lower half looked dark and blocked. Now it was about eleven forty. I moved myself next to his ribs and placed my flat hands in traditional Reiki torso positions. Now it was just before noon.

I quietly asked him, as I softly touched his hairline, to come back to the room. He asked me what I saw. I explained how his lower torso just looked kind of dark.

He explained, "I believe that someone has put something inside of me. I've been cursed. Is that possible?"

I looked at him with eyes of concern. "Yes, that could happen."

He explained the pain on his left side under his rib. I wondered, what organ is that? I asked him if he'd had a doctor check out what was going on and how long it had been like this, suggesting he may want to have a medical person look at it. But I could try something else for now. I was seeing that he needed extraction work and found it interesting he'd been drawn to me. I put more protection around myself, and I removed a black, foggy mass from his body and sent it wrapped up, far away. I thought, *I hope that helps. I wonder if I got all of it.* Then I added back into the fresh void a clear, bright color. I took a deep breath, and I was ready for lunch. So, we headed off to the Kitchen Table.

"Would you like to sit on the table with the group or sit with me on the side?" he asked.

I was delighted my new friend just gave me a choice of eating a meal with him or not. "With you."

I headed to the staff-served buffet to gather my delicious lunch. When I entered the dining room, I saw he had placed us at my favorite table, next to the fireplace. I felt very grateful I got to enjoy this type of interaction.

The Aussie said, "I've spent so much money trying to heal, and you did it just like that?"

He beamed with joy. I hoped it had been a successful healing, since it nagged at me that he needed more.

Soon, our table filled with our familiar gang, and we all planned to join the nature walk on the trails in the campus area. The tour was a mix of selfies with a botanical and history class, and we walked through the forest. The redwoods and bays towered above us. We ate greens from the forest floor, all of us having a great time.

I caught my sister on video as she stood on the amphitheater stage and sang gratitude to the grace of God. The Aussie pounded his chest in the background as she completed her song.

We checked out the cooking school kitchen and gardens, and Josie captured an amazing photo of a bee resting on a purple flower. I tried to hold the flower still for her, but all I did was scare the bee, but she somehow still managed to get a great shot.

Then, we all headed to the café for refreshment and to enjoy our final goodbyes. I could have just stayed, but how would I explain to my ninety-year-old mother I was having too good of a time in Scotts Valley to show up for her birthday?

This time with me driving, my sister and I headed to San Jose in the rental car. She suggested heading to Good Karma, a wonderful vegetarian café with artisan ales. Sitting outside on a Sunday afternoon with no work in sight was a perfect time for an ale and jackfruit tacos. I was in heaven. We reminisced about the class. She shared how happy she was with her new skills.

We headed to the airport, and somehow we both made it onto the same plane. At a few points, I had my doubts, but after I personally handed my sister her boarding pass at the Southwest kiosk, I left her there to go through security and board the plane on her own. She took a while to board, and I was relieved when she did finally join us dead last onto the packed flight.

The man in the seat next to me offered me a book, which I accepted. My nose was draining constantly. Apparently, I was having a delayed allergic reaction to the redwoods. Or maybe my body was purging something else? I constantly wiped my nose with my cotton hooded wrap as I devoured forty-two pages of *Buddha's Map: His Original Teachings on the Awakening, Ease, and Insight in the Heart of Meditation*, written by Doug Kraft, who lived and taught in Sacramento. I was so grateful for it all and for my wonderful life.

CHAPTER 7

Miracles Happen

It was a Thursday night in September 2019, I was a little tired, and the club was crowded. I noticed a man staring at me. I sat down and joined him. His story got interesting fast. He had just flown in from Hawaii at the request of his siblings.

His eighty-year-old father was in the hospital, for a surgery to correct excessive pain caused by something that had happened in the first surgery to repair his hip. The final result was that the man had ended up with a sepsis infection, and now he was in a coma. Otherwise, he had been a healthy eighty-year-old. The accident that had caused the surgeries in the first place had happened when he was up on the roof of his home fixing the weathervane.

I ordered a glass of wine. I needed to slow down a second and just listen. Apparently, the father was wealthy and married to a much younger woman who was consenting to have him taken off life support, claiming it would be what he would want. His children were protesting this.

I listened and decided my point of view, thinking what he had meant when he composed his last wishes was that if he was on life support and there was just no way he was going to recover, then he would like to be taken off life support. I was going to give the wife the benefit of the doubt, thinking she was only misinterpreting his wishes. But understandably, his children were very upset. I analyzed the situation; the series of accidents had put him in a very unfortunate situation, but he wasn't dead, and I had a strong feeling this might be something I could help with. Out of the goodness of my heart, I promised his son that I would go into meditation the next day and have a talk with his dad.

The son texted me from the hospital: "We are battling with his wife; thank God my sister and brother agreed to keep him on life support for at least ninety days."

I answered, "I also agreed that people healed from this infection."

It was Friday afternoon, and I had showered. I was getting ready to walk out the door and find something to eat on my way to work when I remembered my promise. What I had promised to do wasn't a big deal, as talking to sick people in hospitals had been common practice when I studied with the group under Art Runningbear. I was well-practiced with talking to people on the other side, so I went into meditation and traveled metaphysically to the spirit of this man. I found him; he looked like a blue orb on the left side of the hospital room, floating above his body. Also, there were a lot of angels hanging around. I asked them to assist me, and we began healing the body. Then I had a little heart-to-heart talk with the soul or spirit of Mr. Eighty-Year-Old who climbs on roofs to fix weathervanes. I explained to him very bluntly it was time to get back into his body. I told him his youngest son was there and waiting for him to wake up.

He argued with me. "That body is no good; it's shot."

The angels were working quickly now, as I had explained to them about the infection and the importance of getting it out of the body. And then I continued to be bossy with Mr. Eighty-Year-Old, telling him that body only needs his life force back inside of it, and then it would come back to life. I wasn't really giving him much choice, since I was very firm and very assertive. The angels were quite excited and working diligently. They seemed very happy this was all happening. I finished my meditation, and I figured I could go back and talk to him again tomorrow. But now I was really hungry and needed to get to work.

A few minutes later, I was in the drive-thru line at the Pollo Loco when his youngest son's text came through. I'm going to quote this text exactly because I was about as surprised as you are going to be.

Friday, September 13, 6:28 p.m.

My dad just woke up.
PRAISE GOD. I don't know what you did, but it worked.
Thank you from the bottom of my heart!
I love you for what you've done.

My response was, "Oh my God, I just did it? So thankful, so beautiful. I am ruining my make-up, crying."

Then it started, message after message. Two poems, praises that I had so much talent, explaining to me that I was a shaman, telling me he was transferring jobs to move to town. He kept bringing up that he had gifts for me and that his family was going to name a park after me. On the only short phone conversation over the weekend, he told me a friend had told him that knowing someone like me was like knowing a leprechaun, and if you were romantically involved with someone like me, it was like knowing three leprechauns.

This was all making me uncomfortable but, I was keeping in contact with the son, because I was worried about his father. And I continued checking on his father's progress through the weekend. I was glad to hear they had attended Mass at the hospital on Sunday and amazingly, the father was released from the hospital by Monday and doing really well. I was so thankful, and this was so beautiful.

By the end of the weekend, I had needed to explain to the son I was dating someone else and not available for anything romantic. I had also asked him to only communicate with me by email because his text messages were very excessive and beginning to get intrusive, popping up all day and half the night, and interrupting everything I was doing. Well, I didn't respond to emails on Monday night after 11:30 p.m. because I was sleeping. Maybe he imagined someone like me didn't need sleep or something? Anyway, he got very angry and very mean. I really thought this insult was funniest: "If you did this for financial gain, may God help you."

Then he told me it was probably just a fluke, and I didn't even do anything. But that was okay. I knew what I did, and it definitely wasn't to get paid—we had never even discussed any form of pay for me, and it wasn't on my mind. I had acted on my intuition. And judging by the enthusiasm of those angels, I really feel I made the right choice. Honestly, I humbly admit that I am not convinced it wasn't a total coincidence. But the son did write in a poem and said in our phone conversation that his dad told of a blonde angel when he awoke. I don't actually believe his dad told him that, but nonetheless, it all happened.

I'm going to close this story with *I am so grateful.* I listened to a crow. I traveled across the world, dove the Great Barrier Reef, and I spent most of 2019 with my family.

I was finishing up my Clairvoyants 1 course that I had started October of 2019 in San Diego. I had been calling in on FaceTime, but then in March, the whole world shut down. My parents, fearing COVID-19, asked me to stay gone from their home. When I continued in April with Clairvoyants 2, all the classes were now being held on Zoom. So luckily, the change of my geographic location did not interrupt my studies.

I could have ignored the crow's pleas in October 2017 to get out into the world and do healing work.

But I had listened, and I have been so amazingly rewarded, and I didn't miss that opportunity to spend time with my parents and to travel to the other side of the world. It's different now; in fact, the whole world is different. I'm not traveling, for one thing. I've been creating HeartSpirit fragrances, cooking for my close friends, doing yoga at home and at the park. I've been building the Livingnowonline.com website and store, doing energy healing work, and writing.

I'm not immune to the pain of the world. But I'm grateful to all my amazing mentors, who have shown me how I can feel and share the Divine. I have explained how I was shown my abilities as a healer and how the unseen became seen. Truly, I'm very thankful for all my helpers here on earth and those from the other side.

I'm looking forward to getting back out into the world, spreading the light around, enjoying the love and light of others, and sharing more stories. I've found it so enjoyable that my soul has learned to put stories on paper. If I can do this, I truly believe anyone can. Each one of us is a light; hopefully we all can remember that we are all connected.

Please turn off the TV and live together now.

ACKNOWLEDGEMENTS

First and foremost, I want to thank Art Runningbear for waking me up.

Next, I want to express my gratitude to Diane and Terry for being present as I opened my eyes.

Also, I want to send sincere love all my teachers, classmates, and students from Intuitive Insights for giving me constant support throughout the whole process of creating this story.

Most importantly, I want to thank all four of my editors, the two photographers, my graphic designer, and my book designer, for all their patience with me as I fumbled through the process of creating a published book. Without any one of them, I would not have been able to complete this task.

Finally, I'm so grateful to the Source for allowing it all to happen.

With gratitude I write,

Spirit instructed me to write this book to show people a different way to live.

I don't know which came first, the chicken or the egg. Also, I don't know as seekers, if we are chickens or eggs. Only as a spiritual teacher, I feel I am an embryo growing within the yolk.

To sincerely show my gratitude to my fellow seekers, may you be conscious or unconscious, I've created a special gift of a guided, heart-centering, grounding meditation.

Available at:
Livingnowonline.com
Please join me there now.
I'm excited to hear if and how you are enjoying or enjoyed this memoir.

Thank you,

Susie*
The Dyslexic Healer